IMAGES
of England

AROUND
BURNOPFIELD

Tell me not, ye hoary sages,
Of the dark, the bygone ages;
Tell me not of other climes,
Darkened with the foulest crimes.

Talk ye of learning spreading wide,
Of science taking giant strides,
High-ton'd morals, manners refined,
Leaving all former days behind.

Talk ye of intellect's proud march,
Its flights sublime, its deep research,
Reforms, improvements without end,
But sure enough there's room to mend.

Had I the power, I would unfold
A tale, dark as was ever told,
A crime of deepest, blackest hue,
Yet no more black, alas, than true.

A youth of learning and of skill,
Who nobly did his station fill,
To rapine falls a sacrifice,
And by the hands of ruffians dies.

A youth of worth, and spotless name,
Who might have scal'd the heights of fame,
His father's joy, his mother's pride,
In life's fresh bloom, thus sadly died.

Far from his home he met his fate
A fate how dreadful to relate;
No friend was near, no pitying eye
To witness his last agony.

Perhaps with joy his soul beat high,
Nor knew he that his end was nigh,
Perhaps bright hope his breast inspired,
When that sad fatal shot was fired.

Fraudless and unsuspecting he
Nor knew, nor feared, an enemy,
The cowardly assassin fired,
He fell, he groan'd and soon expired.

The cowardly assassins then
(I cannot, will not, call them men,
But fiends in human shape they be,
Full types of the great enemy.)

Their victims welt'ring in his blood
They seized and dragg'd into the wood,
And what doth make their crime still worse,
They mangled his poor, lifeless corpse.

They then dispoiled the injured dead,
They took his watch, his purse and fled;
They thus their murder'd victim left,
Of life and property bereft.

Not in the gloom of thickest night,
When nature's curtain veils from sight,
But in the broad, bright blaze of noon,
This dark, infernal deed was done.

O! ye, who did this wicked deed,
Who made that mother's heart to bleed,
Who fill'd that father's heart with woe,
And laid that youth of promise low.

Your crime is great, of deepest hue,
Heaven's curse rests on your branded brow,
Your shirts are stain'd with guiltless blood,
And scorn'd by men, abhorr'd by God.

You may escape from justice here,
But still the reckoning day draws near,
And suffer for this crime you must,
One day or other; God is just.

Sacred is life, the gift of God,
A precious boon on man bestowed,
Heav'n gives our life, appoints our day,
And curs'd is he who takes away.

O! curs'd lust of paltry gold,
Parent of miseries untold,
For love of thee, ah strange to say,
Man takes his fellow's life away.

Unhappy youth, thee we lament,
Thus to the grave untimely sent,
We hope in peace thy soul doth rest.
Where wicked men no more molest.

Lines on the Murder of Dr Robert Stirling, 1 November 1855, by John Stokoe, blacksmith, of Burnopfield (see page 64).

2

IMAGES
of England

AROUND
BURNOPFIELD

Compiled by
John Uren
from the records of Jack Uren

TEMPUS

First published 2000
Copyright © John Uren, 2000

Tempus Publishing Limited
The Mill, Brimscombe Port,
Stroud, Gloucestershire, GL5 2QG

ISBN 0 7524 1514 X

Typesetting and origination by
Tempus Publishing Limited
Printed in Great Britain by
Midway Clark Printing, Wiltshire

A postcard from Burnopfield, *c.* 1910, showing (clockwise from the top left) a steam train passing through Crookgate, the commemorative fountain on Rowlands Gill bank, the interior of St James' church, Burnopfield Co-operative Society manager's house, Pont Burn bridge, the footbridge over the East Dene, and the coachman's house outside Burnopfield House.

Contents

Acknowledgements

The information used in this book has been derived from two main sources. First, from the extensive personal collection accumulated by Jack Uren and second, from material very kindly supplied by many individuals connected with Burnopfield in some way. It is with very grateful thanks, therefore, that the references from which the book has been compiled together with the names of those who have contributed to its production in any way are acknowledged below.

Publications

Anon, *Burnopfield Gospel Fellowship Fortieth Anniversary, 1948-1988, Commemorative Booklet*; T. Baker, *Burnopfield Cricket Club – A Review of the Post-war Years*, 1974; N. Spence Galbraith, *Dr John Watson (1790/91-1847) of Burnopfield and his assistant Dr John Snow*, Durham County Local History Series, Bulletin 57, pages 32- 50, May 1998; D. Hutt, *Leap Mill: A Guide to the Mill and Farm*, 1994; W. McKie, *The St John Ambulance Brigade Burnopfield Division 1907-1977*; T. Middleton, 'The Lintz Green Murder', in *Back Track*, vol. 5, no. 6, pp. 293-295, Nov./Dec. 1991; F.G. Newman and the Sunniside and District History Society, *Byermoor, Marley Hill and Sunniside*, in the Archive Photographs Series published by the Chalford Publishing Company, ISBN 0 7524 1046 6; Mark Peel, *Cricketing Cavalier – a biography of Colin Milburn*, ISBN 0 233990 26 7; R. Powton, *History of Burnopfield*; J.F. Robinson, *Lintzford, Lintz Green, Chopwell, etc.*; *The History of Burnopfield*; *The Rate of Wages about Burnopfield one hundred and forty years ago*; *An Old Colliery Pay-Sheet*; *The Busty Seam*; A. Spearman & K. Wood, *Leazes Junior Mixed and Infant School 1894-1968 – Past, Present and Future?*; Surtees, *History and Antiquities of Durham*, 1820; J. Uren, '*200 Years of Methodism in Burnopfield – Haswell Memorial Methodist Church 1775-1975, Bicentenary Brochure*, 1975; F. Whellan & Co., *History, Topography and Directory of the County Palatine of Durham*, second edition, 1894; Whickham Local History Class, *History of Whickham*, 1961; Jack Hair and Alan Harrison, *Around Stanley* in the Archive Photographs Series published by the Chalford Publishing Company. ISBN 0 7524 0794 5; Winlaton and District Local History Society, *The Derwent Valley Walk*, a historical guide published by Gateshead Metropolitan Borough Council, 1980.

Individuals

Betty Baker, Doris Baker, Mel and Helen Beadling, Brenda Binnie, Percy Brown, Robert Brown, Sam and Elsie Byfield, Jackie and Judith Forster, Alison Griffin, Dorothy Hall, Ken Hall, Bill Hewison, Bob and Maureen Jackson, Jimmy and Pauline McConnen, Billy McKie, Terry Middleton OBE, Bertha Milburn, Margaret Moss, Philip Murphy, Francis Newman, Noble Parker, Brenda Robson, Pam Small, Bert Yard, John Rymaszewski.

Finally, I would like to thank Tiffany Reed and David Buxton of Tempus Publishing Ltd for very kindly agreeing to publish the book and for their gentle cajoling over the years, without which it would never have been completed.

Introduction

This book has been many years in the preparation. It has been compiled from the numerous books, documents and photographs collected by my father Jack Uren during his lifetime. Christened John but always called Jack, he was a very keen local historian who was well known in the area from his days as a headmaster and from the hundreds of talks he gave to many local and regional organizations over the years. His portfolio ranged from Methodism to pub signs but, despite having been born at Lintz, his greatest love was Burnopfield and it was always his ambition to produce a book on its history. Sadly, having done much of the groundwork, he was unable to complete the task and, after his death on 13 August 1997, I volunteered to finish the job. Initially, I set myself a target date of spring 1999 in order to have the book ready for the new millennium. Little did I know what I'd let myself in for! With hindsight, given the vast amount of material to sift through, this was an improbable completion date. Tragically, it became an impossible one when my mother, Lilian, died very suddenly almost exactly one year after my father on 22 August 1998. Inevitable delays occurred and it was some time before I was able to resume the work in earnest. Nevertheless, with much understanding from my wife Rosemary and our children John and Helen, I managed to restart the project and it is with considerable relief that the task is now finished.

It is important to define this book. It is not meant to be the definitive history of the Burnopfield area (although I am sure that would make a fascinating story); it is simply my father's personal version of its history based on the interests he had in life. These were centred on his long career in teaching, his strong links with Methodism and, above all, his love of the area in which he lived for almost ninety years. These interests were reflected in the records he kept and the book, in turn, is a reflection of those records. Regrettably, due to space restrictions, omissions have been necessary. Difficult decisions had to be made regarding which photographs to include and perhaps the most difficult of all was the decision not to include any information about Gibside, another of my father's passions. To do so would have meant restricting other sections of the book and, as there is already excellent information about Gibside to be had at the National Trust gift shop beside Gibside Chapel, it seemed to be the least painful alternative.

Burnopfield as we now know it covers a much larger area than the Burnopfield of bygone days. References to it in the early eighteenth century show that at that time it only stretched from Busty Bank and Sheephill in the east to The Fold and Bryan's Leap in the west, a distance of a quarter of a mile or so. These four places had then a small cluster of cottages each, and are the oldest parts of the village. There were also two or three small farmsteads and an occasional house by the side of the only road through the village, then called the Lobley Hill Turnpike, which went on to Medomsley. Exactly how long the village has been in existence is difficult to say. Unlike nearby Byermoor, it is not mentioned in Bishop Pudsey's *Bolden Book* of 1183, which is often considered to be Durham's equivalent of the *Domesday Book*. There is evidence to suggest, however, that people have lived in the Burnopfield area for over 400 years. The reasons why the village was originally located where it is are also unclear. The usual ones such as having a Roman connection or being near to a religious settlement or even lying close to a river, do not apply. At first glance, therefore, Burnopfield appears to have no reason for its existence. However, while it is difficult to determine exactly when and why Burnopfield originated, the reasons why it has continued to exist and has developed in the way it has are much more obvious. These can be summed up in the two words 'coal' and 'waggonways', which are discussed later.

Over the years, because of its position, Burnopfield could only expand eastwards and westwards. This it has done by absorbing many of the villages and hamlets around it into its postal district and by allowing council and private housing estates to take up most of its available building land. Burnopfield at the dawn of the twenty-first century has changed out of all recognition from its old waggonway days. However, the most dramatic change of all has been in the occupation of its work force. Since the closure of the local mines and finally all the coastal pits in the early 1990s, there are no miners living in Burnopfield, an unimaginable thought a hundred years ago. Industrial estates, factories, offices and shops now provide employment for both men and women. With the growth of cars and buses, walking to work is almost unheard of and the once great adventure of descending (and ascending!) Rowlands Gill bank to catch the train to Newcastle and Whitley Bay is nowadays remembered by very few of its inhabitants. Fortunately, in spite of its growth, Burnopfield still retains much of its early charm. With its panoramic views of the Derwent Valley and being within easy commuting distance of Newcastle, it is now a very popular residential village.

Compiling this book from my father's records has been a labour of love, which has taught me so much that I never knew about the area in which I grew up. The area has a proud history based largely on the fact that it was the source of some of the best coal in England, much of which ended up warming the people of London. I hope that you will find the book interesting, that it will stimulate you to visit some of the places mentioned and perhaps cause you to look at the area in a different light. My greatest wish, however, is that my mother and father would have liked it, for it is a record of their time and has been written in their memory.

John Uren
June 2000

One
Coal and Waggonways

Although coal was probably mined in north-western County Durham before the fourteenth century, its trade began in earnest in the seventeenth century, with the discovery in the area of large deposits of high quality domestic coal, which was much in demand. Ironically, the Great Fire of London in 1666 further fuelled this demand when brick houses with purpose-built chimneys replaced the hundreds of wooden houses destroyed by the flames. At first, the coal outcrops near the Tyne were worked since the hewn coal could easily be transported from the coal staithes by shallow-draft boats known as 'keels' to larger sailing ships moored at the mouth of the Tyne. However, as workings became exhausted, collieries were opened further away from the river and transporting the coal to the staithes became more of a problem. Initially, horses and carts were used but these proved to be slow and expensive. A cheaper, quicker solution was found with the development of wooden railways along which wooden waggons were drawn by horses. By the end of the seventeenth century, many of these so-called 'waggonways' had been laid throughout the coal mining areas of the North of England.

Because of its position, Burnopfield was found to be an ideal place for the waggonways from the Pontop and Tanfield Moor areas to pass through on their way to the staithes. Two waggonways in particular, one passing near Bryan's Leap and the other down Busty Bank, were important in the development of Burnopfield. These two waggonways, converging at either end of the village, and the work provided by the many small pits in and around the Bryan's Leap area, as indicated on a map drawn up in 1719, were the main reasons for the growth and development of Burnopfield. The drivers of the waggons were often local farmers and their grown-up sons who usually kept a few horses 'to go to the waggons', and the money they earned helped to pay the rent for their farms. However, it was hard work and few fortunes were made. The distance between the colliery and the staithes was known as a 'gate' and a man and his horse could usually do one and a half gates in a day. In 1723 the going rate for the Pontop to Derwenthaugh 'gate' was 2s 3d so a day's pay would have been 3s 4½d.

Burnopfield viewed from Byermoor church, 2000. Burnopfield is built on a long narrow shelf. The higher ground of Hobson, on the left, slopes down and then levels out to take in Burnopfield before descending rapidly into the Derwent valley, on the right. On this shelf, never more than 300 yards wide, the village has grown to a considerable size, in spite of the fact that development has only been possible to the east and the west.

In 1960, when the last of the old houses on The Fold near Bryan's Leap was being demolished, a stone lintel above the fireplace, bearing the inscription 'J.H. 1669', was found. The initials were those of John Harrison, a member of a Byermoor family that was active in the coal trade. Records show that he was baptized on 29 January 1633 and was buried on 22 April 1710. His father, Richard Harrison, had inherited the house from his own mother in the sixteenth century. Hence, people have lived in the Bryan's Leap area for over 400 years. The lintel was removed and placed above the fireplace of a new house built in the 1960s on the same site by a Mr Grundy.

Birch Crescent, 2000. The first waggonway of any significance to pass through Burnopfield was probably built around 1700 and was known as the Main Way. It originated in the Pontop area, picking up coal from Dipton, Mountsett, Tantobie and Lintz Colliery. Between Lintz Colliery and the Leazes School there was a pond for soaking the waggons' wooden wheels to prevent them from splitting. After crossing the Syke Road, it ran down the valley in which Birch Crescent was built.

The dirt road at the bottom of the allotments near West View, 2000. The Main Way ran along this route before passing another pond near the old Brewery Yard, which also supplied the brewery with water at a later date.

The Fold area opposite Eddie Foster's old corner shop, *c.* 1950. Near here was the point at which the Main Way crossed the Lobley Hill turnpike.

The West Dene below the Fold area, 2000. The Main Way took a precipitous route across the West Dene and on down Rowlands Gill bank. It crossed the Derwent on a wooden bridge known as the Cowford Bridge (to the east of the present road bridge) before continuing on to Derwenthaugh. The Cowford Bridge took a terrible pounding as the waggons reached high speeds on their journey down the hill, and records show that frequent repairs were required. The Bryan's Leap to Derwenthaugh waggonway was the most costly that had then been built, with the construction work on Rowlands Gill bank and the filling-in of the denes being the most difficult ever undertaken in the coal trade at that time.

The site of the 'Keelman's Bridge', c. 1900. Tradition has it that some out-of-work Tyne keelmen built a bridge across the East Dene to provide a shunting area for the coal waggons. This is probably true, as it is very likely that the keelmen would undertake work that would help to bring more trade to the Tyne. Two of the pillars of the original Keelman's Bridge still stand and now carry a footbridge over the dene.

Top of Busty Bank, c. 1890. The second waggonway of significance to Burnopfield came from pits in the Tanfield Moor and Hobson areas, and was probably made between 1750 and 1763. It followed a track at a slightly lower level than the old Pontop and Jarrow railway, passing to the east of Burnopfield House, reaching the top of Busty Bank near an old blacksmith's shop. It continued down the bank, meeting the Main Way near the present road junction beside Leap Mill Farm. In relatively recent history, locals still used to refer to Busty Bank as the 'Old Waggonway'.

The Blacksmith's shop at the top of Busty Bank, *c.* 1880.

Each waggon held a 'chaldron' of coal (about 53cwt) and two sets of rails were laid along the route. The down track carried the full waggons on double layered rails so that the top rail could be replaced easily when it had worn out. The up track carried the empty waggons on single layered rails. The waggons, rails and sleepers were made of hardwood, with the wheels being formed from planks. Beech rails were often used and the huge demand for replacement rails may be the reason why so many beech trees can still be found in nearby Gibside Wood and in the denes of Burnopfield. It would never have been imagined at the beginning of the seventeenth century that iron would take over.

Two

Burnopfield

As the coal trade developed, so did Burnopfield. Service industries associated with the waggonways began to spring up, such as wood dealers and mechanics. By 1775 it had a Methodist chapel and several places to drink. In the Bryan's Leap area there were a brewery and four public houses: the Black Horse Inn, the Sun Inn, the Grapes Inn and the Brewers' Arms. In the Busty Bank area there was a brewery behind Burnopfield House and two public houses: the Queen's Head and the Burton House. Only the Sun Inn and the Burton House still carry on their original trade. The Black Horse Inn has been converted into flats, the Brewers' Arms was demolished, the Grapes Inn became Bourne House at No. 3 Dene View and the Queen's Arms became Wrenvue at No. 14 Busty Bank. Both breweries have also gone. The one at Bryan's Leap was converted into a group of small dwelling houses, which became known as The Brewery Yard, and the brewery behind Burnopfield House became a Mechanics' Institute, one of a number set up nationally to promote the general education of the people. The first lecture given was by a Mr Muir on astronomy around the time of the eclipse of the sun on 15 May 1836. Over the years, the Institute proved to be very successful. Later, however, the building fell into disuse and was pulled down.

Developments in Burnopfield increased rapidly with the formation of the Co-operative Movement in the 1860s, and between 1895 and 1914, a considerable amount of improvement work was undertaken in Burnopfield. New houses, shops, roads and footpaths were constructed. Existing houses were repaired. Drainage and sanitation were improved and water was piped directly into homes for the first time. The cleaning of ash pits and outside toilets was improved as were sewerage and sewage disposal. Gas and electric street lighting became commonplace, with gas supplied by the Busty Bank Gas Company, located near the bottom of Busty Bank on the right-hand side, and electricity by Burnopfield Co-operative Society. This was indeed a time of significant change in Burnopfield. Sadly, however, some things never change, as this report of 1914 shows: 'Considerable damage has been done to the public street lamps by the wilful damage of glasses etc. A reward of £5 has been offered for information leading to a conviction.'

Numbers 30 and 32 Front Street, Burnopfield, are in the oldest part of the village and were built around 1690. Number 30 is reputed to have its own ghost – a mysterious and totally benevolent grey lady who flits by the window but never goes inside the house. A cross and a rose are cut into one of its walls and a tombstone is built into another. The houses are reputed to have been built by a sailor named Shafto who decided to walk inland from South Shields as far as he could and then to build a house at the spot where he could walk no further. Number 32 has a window above the front door behind which Shafto is supposed to have sat and watched the ships out at sea through his telescope.

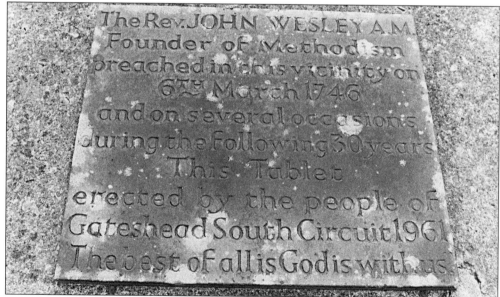

The inscription on the Wesley Memorial in the garden of No. 28 Sheephill, near to where John Wesley preached on 5 March 1746. Wesley records this visit in his Journal as follows: 'I preached in Whickham at noon; in the evening at Spen; the next day at Burnopfield.' He preached in the village on at least a dozen occasions and, from his journal entries, it seems to have occupied a very warm place in his heart.

Burnopfield Methodists holding a service at the Wesley Memorial, Sheephill, in 1983. From left to right: George Caisley, Joan Caisley, Eunice Charlton, Millie Brown, Brian Charlton, Lilian Uren, Billy Teasdale, Revd Rufus Booth, Cynthia Ashmole. The memorial was erected on 24 May (Wesley Day) 1961.

The original 1775 Wesleyan Methodist chapel, which was built by members of a Methodist Society formed as a result of Wesley's visits. This was the first place of worship in the village. It faced east and west and was built by a stonemason named William Bickerton who lived, rather appropriately, in Sheephill. There was also a caretaker's cottage and a stable for the preacher's horse. The stone staircase led to an upper room that, from about 1820, was used as a day school. One of the schoolmasters, George Todd, had a wooden leg, which kept getting stuck in the rotten floor. To release him, his pupils had to go into the stable below and push his stump up with a broom.

View along Front Street towards Crookgate, *c.* 1850. Grove Terrace had not yet been built.

Grove Terrace United Methodist Free Church, *c.* 1900, showing Burnopfield Co-op in the background and the blacksmith's shop at the top of Busty Bank. The Co-operative Hall had not yet been built. Members of Burnopfield Wesleyan church who had become dissatisfied with the Wesleyan Movement built this church in 1870. It could seat 250 and cost £600, and its members adopted the name United Methodists. Underneath it was a Hall, which also served as a school. The Grove church closed some years ago and is now owned by a company that imports watch straps.

Burnopfield Haswell Memorial Methodist church, c. 1900. By 1879, the old Wesleyan church was badly in need of repair. It was rebuilt on the same site and opened in 1880 with seating for 350 at a cost of £560. It was named in memory of Revd John Partis Haswell, a Wesleyan minister who been converted in the old church in 1808. In latter years, the building was simply referred to as Burnopfield Methodist church to avoid confusion with the village of Haswell to the east of Durham city.

The interior of the Burnopfield Haswell Memorial church, c. 1906. The original pulpit from which Wesley had preached was taken out of the 1775 church and bought, together with a pane of glass from the window beneath the pulpit, by a Mr Thomas Liddle of Grove House, Burnopfield. On this pane was the inscription 'Preach the Word, Paul to Timothy', which had been scratched on the glass on 3 December 1780 by Revd Samuel Bardsley, a close friend of John Wesley's, who had been preaching in the church on that day. What became of these relics is not known.

The Wesley Hall, c. 1970. This multi-purpose building was opened behind Burnopfield Methodist church on 24 November 1906. In 1980, as a result of the closure of the Grove Terrace and Hobson Methodist chapels, the Wesley Hall was extended to include a Grove-Hobson room in which some of the church services were held. During the building of this extension, a bottle was found in a wall cavity containing a copy of *The Newcastle Daily Chronicle* and various other documents. The bottle and its contents were restored to the cavity during the building of the extension. Sadly, the Wesley Hall was demolished in 2000.

Some of the 'Merry Optimists', c. 1940. These were a group of entertainers based in the Wesley Hall who gave concerts and recitals in the area. In one eight-month period they gave over 100 concerts. Their members included Elsie Churcher, Walter Churcher, Bertha Davis, Harold Potts, Jenny Potts (seated on the right), Nan Seth and Norman Seth.

Burnopfield Methodist Church Youth Club, 1964. From left to right, back row: Terry Macnally, Barty Hall, Howard Guy, John Uren, Susan Hudspith, Eileen Johnson, Jean Milburn, Glynis Parr, Robin Rispin, Tony Gibson, Donald Cooper, Alan Watson. Middle row: Alan Brewis, Maureen Brewis, Neil Herdman, Len Hinds, Brian Shield, David McKie, -?-, Margaret Chapman, Pauline ?. Front row: Sandy Mearns, Hilda Guy, Revd Thomas Guy, Joan Caisley, John Herdman. Sitting on the ground: Barbara Draper, -?-, Glynis Johnson.

A Burnopfield Methodist church production of *Aladdin* given in the Wesley Hall, February 1966, with Brian Charlton as Aladdin. Brian later became headmaster of Burnopfield Junior and Infants' School.

The site of the Burnopfield Methodist church, 2000. The church and the Wesley Hall were demolished in 2000 after the buildings had been condemned. They are being replaced with a smaller building that will be easier to maintain. The last service held in the church was the funeral of Maurice Churcher on Thursday 4 March 1993. Maurice was the organist at the church for many years and also wrote several pantomimes that were performed in the Wesley Hall. There used to be four thriving Methodist churches in the area; sadly only Burnopfield remains with a membership of just fifty or so. It is difficult to believe that, just like the mining community, the once vibrant Methodist community has all but disappeared.

The Grapes Inn viewed from Sheephill, c. 1880. The building on the left is Roddam's house, which later became the Victory Club. The Grapes Inn is now Bourne House, No. 3 Dene View. In 1719, it was a detached building supplying nails for the collieries and the waggonways. As an inn, it was a stagecoach stop for the horse-drawn coach service between Gateshead and Stanhope, which opened on Monday 1 August 1834. Between 1816 and 1858, Thomas Rippon, a cabinet maker and engraver, lived at the Grapes Inn. In 1818 he made an oak chair from the original beams of Blanchland Abbey, which is still on view in the abbey today. Ironically, between 1899 and 1984, the former Grapes Inn was used as a Methodist manse.

Front Street, Burnopfield, c. 1960, showing the Victory Club on the right (the white building) and Andy Eltringham's old barber's shop next to the old fish and chip shop.

Dr Grensill's house, at the head of the West Dene, c. 1950. In the early nineteenth century, the Brewers' Arms, which was a veranda-type building, became the home of a Dr Grensill who set up a practice there. It was occasionally used by the Catholics for Mass, which was said by Father Patrick Thomas Mathews, who later founded Byermoor Sacred Heart church. It was eventually demolished in the 1960s.

Hannah Hopper's Yard, next to the Verandah House, *c.* 1940.

The site of the old veranda house at the head of the West Dene, 1975. The white building on the left is the Black Horse Inn, which was converted into flats in 1991.

The site of the old Brewery Yard, 1979. Several families lived here, as well as Janey Lamb who had a small shop tucked away in one corner. The Brewery Yard was finally demolished in 1961, the last family to leave being that of Mr Isaac Kendall in 1960. All that remains now is a rectangular plot of grass-covered land.

Some of the children who lived in the Brewery Yard, c. 1950.

The first post office in the village at No. 1 Derwent View, *c.* 1840. In February 1834 a daily postal service from Gateshead to Burnopfield was established.

Burnopfield post office staff, *c.* 1950.

Burnopfield Co-operative Store, Front Street, c. 1910. Originally part of Blaydon District Industrial and Provident Society, the members of Burnopfield Co-op formed an independent society in 1889. The store was a focal point of the village for many years. Initially, it dealt in provisions and drapery, then butchery and boot and shoe departments were opened and later still a new hall and several cottages were built. This established Burnopfield as a shopping centre for the mining families in the neighbouring villages, many of whom became members of the Co-op with their own dividend number.

Burnopfield Co-op employees, c. 1900. Co-op members were encouraged to save and buy their own homes and new streets of houses were built to accommodate this demand. Branches of Burnopfield Co-operative Society were opened at Rowlands Gill, Leazes, The Fell, Hookergate, Highfield, Hobson and Sunniside. Traces of the Rowlands Gill branch can still be seen inscribed on some of the stonework at the top of the old building. The Burnopfield shop finally closed on 12 January 1985 when it was part of Towneley Co-operative Society.

The former Co-op store manager's house, built by Henry Curry-Wood, later Alderman Curry-Wood, who was the first general manager of Burnopfield Co-operative Society. In around 1915, Tanfield Lea Secondary School was renamed Alderman Wood School after him.

A Burnopfield Co-op horse-drawn van, c. 1910.

The area around the top of Busty Bank, *c.* 1910. The Grove Terrace church now has a front porch and an extension for a Sunday School and a caretaker's house. The small buildings in the centre of the photograph were shops.

One of the shops which used to stand near the site of the present council-owned Communal Hall, or 'The Hut' as it is known locally. Before The Hut was built, Jack Davidson used to have a barber's shop in one of the shops in this area.

The former Walter Willson's shop, Busty Bank, c. 1920.

Athletics at Burnopfield Flower Show, c. 1950. In 1873, the first Burnopfield Flower Show took place in a field in the Bryan's Leap area, to the right of Sandypath Lane, behind The Fold, when the Winlaton Band entertained the crowds. The show was held annually by the Burnopfield Floral, Horticultural and Agricultural Society as a means of encouraging amateur gardeners. It ran successfully for many years, celebrating its Diamond Jubilee in 1933.

Burnopfield Silver Band in 1925. They used to play at Burnopfield Flower Show.

Burnopfield viewed from Dyke Heads, *c.* 1900, with Byermoor church and colliery in the background.

Looking along Front Street from the corner near the Sun Inn, *c.* 1950. The small corrugated iron building on the right near the present bus stop was a cobbler's shop. The road to the left, which runs down to Rowlands Gill, was for many years shown on maps as the 'New Road'. The first section ran from the Sun Inn down the hill to where the commemorative fountain now stands. Here it met the second section that ran from where the cenotaph now stands down the hill to the Busty Bank junction beside Leap Mill Farm. The work commenced in July 1900 and the new road was opened to the public on 28 August 1901.

Burnopfield furniture removers, *c.* 1900.

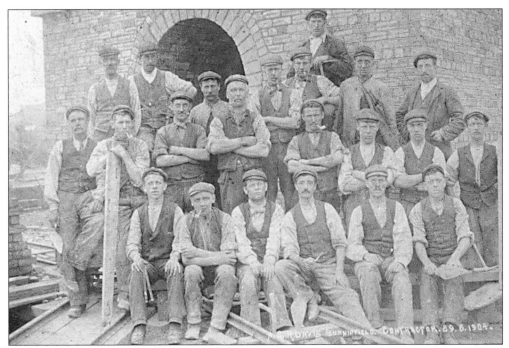

Some of the employees of A. & R. Davis in 1904. The Davises were well-known local builders towards the end of the nineteenth and beginning of the twentieth centuries. They built many places in the village including the Hobson Methodist chapel (1890), the Leazes Board School (1894) and the Wesley Hall (1906).

Bob Davidson's horse and trap in 1909. He used it to provide a 'taxi' service in the village.

The opening of Burnopfield ambulance station in 1909, showing Dyke Heads in the background. In 1903, following the occurrence of a few accidents in the area, one or two prominent citizens decided that an Ambulance Brigade should be formed. Doctor and Mrs Wynne Boland were great benefactors to this cause and allowed their home to be used for instruction in first aid. The first flower show organized to raise funds was held in the field adjoining Leazes Hall by courtesy of Major Shield who was in residence there at that time. The Burnopfield Division of the St John Ambulance Brigade was officially enrolled on 16 February 1907. The funds for the original building, which cost £200, and a horse-drawn ambulance, which cost £100, were raised by a combination of door-to-door collections of a penny per week and by miners in the local collieries agreeing to have a penny per week deducted from their wages. Mrs Mary Watson of Burnopfield House generously donated land on which to build and her daughter Miss Mabel Watson officially opened the new building on 14 August 1909. It comprised a doctor's room and an ambulance house for the horse-drawn ambulance.

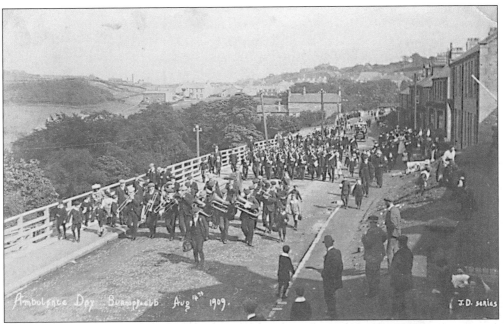

Burnopfield Ambulance Brigade parading along Front Street, 14 August 1909.

The original horse-drawn ambulance, c. 1910. When it was called out, a horse had to be borrowed from the local Co-op or from one of the nearby collieries. At that time, Burnopfield was the only village in the North of England to have its own ambulance station for the general public. Nursing utensils for use in the home were available to the public free of charge on the production of a doctor's note.

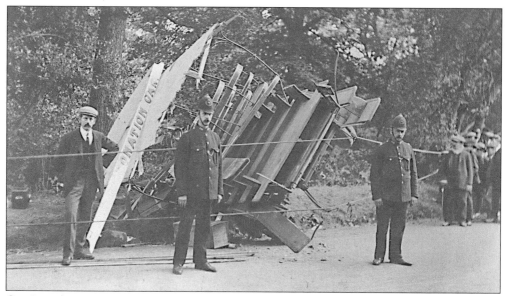

On Saturday 26 August 1911, a loaded charabanc, known as a Coronation Car, carrying members of the Consett Co-operative Choir from Consett to an annual contest at Prudhoe, crashed into a tree on Medomsley Bank when its brakes failed. Nine of the choir were killed instantly and a tenth died shortly afterwards; many others were injured. Members of the Burnopfield Ambulance Brigade, who had been attending their annual flower show and sports day in Thompson's field at Bryan's Leap, got into the shafts of their horse-drawn ambulance and manhandled it to Medomsley Bank while someone fetched a horse.

In the early 1950s, the ambulance station was completely refurbished and another storey was added. This increased the accommodation to include a lecture room, a recreation room and kitchen facilities. The refurbished building was re-opened in a grand ceremony by the then County Commissioner, Sir Miles Wayman, on 26 September 1953. Burnopfield Tennis Club can be seen in the background. The Club was formed in 1911 and its first courts were at Roseberry Cottage near the top of Syke Bank.

Members of the Burnopfield Ambulance Brigade at the opening of the extension in 1953.

Members of the Burnopfield Ambulance Brigade Ladies' Committee, c. 1960. From left to right, back row: Mrs Joan Caisley, Mrs Largue, Mrs Gibson, Mrs Jean McKie, Mrs Charlton, Mrs Doreen Dodd. Front row: Mrs K. Caisley, Mrs Wood, Mrs Bainbridge, Mrs Hedworth, Mrs Hedworth's sister, Mrs E. Tinnion, Mrs Liddle.

Burnopfield St John Nursing Cadets, c. 1960.

Charles ('Charlie') Metcalf (left) and Billy McKie, long-standing members of Burnopfield Ambulance Brigade, c. 1970. On Friday 16 July 1965, Billy McKie and two other miners were trapped by a serious fall of stone at Byermoor Colliery. Charlie Metcalf, also a miner at the colliery, was a member of the rescue team who went to their aid. Two of the men were brought out quickly but Billy McKie was very badly injured and trapped. With no thought for his own safety, Charlie Metcalf slithered and crawled his way through falling debris, dust and loose rock on two occasions to administer morphine to his friend to ease his pain. Billy McKie was eventually freed and taken to hospital in Newcastle where an urgent operation was carried out. Despite a broken arm, head injuries and twenty-three broken ribs, he made a full recovery. As a result of his heroic actions, Charlie Metcalf was awarded the St John Life-saving Medal at a special ceremony on 26 March 1966, a very rare honour.

The commemorative drinking fountain, *c.* 1910. In 1906, a drinking fountain for people and horses was erected at the junction on the Rowlands Gill road where the road from the Sun Inn meets the road from the war memorial. It is made of red polished granite and is inscribed as follows: 'Erected by Miss M.A. Rippon in remembrance of her brother William C. Rippon, of his life's residence in Burnopfield and in kindness to dumb animals 1906. The donor of this fountain died 3rd Octr. before its completion.' It was unveiled by Mr Henry Curry-Wood, the manager of Burnopfield Co-operative Society. In 1995, it was restored thanks to the efforts of Tot Cheeseman. Sadly, however, it has again been vandalized.

Front Street, Burnopfield, *c.* 1910. On the left, the gable end of the Sun Inn can be seen. The Black Horse is set back on the opposite side of the road. The large square building on the right served as a storehouse for the Brewers' Arms, the roof of which can be seen just behind it to the right.

The first occupants of the Aged Miners' Homes, 1924. The homes were opened on 2 February of that year.

Burnopfield Cenotaph, *c.* 1930. In 1914, when the First World War broke out, a large number of volunteers went from Burnopfield, many of them never to return. After the war, in 1919, a public subscription was made to provide a memorial to the fallen. This was built in 1920, being officially opened by Councillor J. Trotter, the then Chairman of Tanfield UDC, on 29 January 1921. The response to the public appeal was so good that sufficient cash remained after the erection of the memorial to purchase a motor ambulance for the Ambulance Brigade to replace the horse-drawn one.

Members of Burnopfield WI in April 1965, when they provided the entertainment at the Golden Jubilee meeting. Those dressed as Queens of Bygone Days are, from left to right, Mrs G. Stanwick as Queen Mary, Mrs J. Uren as Queen Elizabeth, Mrs E. Potts as Queen Victoria, Mrs J. Cooper as Queen Anne, and Mrs C. Cerr as Queen Mary II. The ladies on the right are Millie Brown, Bertha Burns, Marion Nelson, Kitty Shaw, Ella White, -?-, Isabel Cowans. Burnopfield WI was formed in 1936. Lintz and Hobson also had WIs but they both closed several years ago, having found it difficult to get ladies to fill the official positions. Some of their members joined Burnopfield WI while others joined the Tanfield branch.

Members of Burnopfield WI giving a show in the Wesley Hall at their group meeting on 29 October 1985. From left to right, back row: Irene Watson, Irene Fearon, Joyce Williams. Front row: Brenda Robson, Cynthia Peacock, Jean Cousins, Christine Jewel, Alice Stewart, Doris Tinnion, Jen Taylor, Jean Thompson.

The Dene Fisheries on Front Street, Burnopfield, *c.* 1980. This old pitch pine shack was built in 1922, four years before Harry Ramsden's fish and chip shop at Guiseley in Yorkshire. Next door used to be Andy Eltringham's barber's shop, which later became a fruit and veg shop before it burned down in 1985.

The current owners of the Dene Fisheries, Mel and Helen Beadling, who kept the old shack going while they built a fine new stone building next to it on the site of the old fruit and veg shop. The old shack was finally demolished in 1995 after more than seventy years of faithful service and an unimaginable number of chips!

Burnopfield Park, *c.* 1940, before the present bowls pavilion and the houses on Birch Crescent were built. Opened in June 1939, Burnopfield Park originally contained a bowling green, a putting green and some tennis courts. The putting green was converted into an adventure playground in 1986, which was opened by the athlete Kirsty Wade, but this has now been removed.

The Burnopfield Park ladies' bowling team, *c.* 1965.

Burnopfield Park men's bowling team, 1990. From left to right, back row: Harry Holcroft, Keith Anderson, Bob Temperley, Billy Scorer, Les Elliott, Ramsey Lawson, Vince Watson, Keith Hartley, Archie Dodd. Middle row: Bob Robinson, Bob Foster, Tommy Howe, Bill Milburn, Frank Clark, Jack Davison, Cyril Turner, Gibbie Rowland, D. Lamour, Hammel Harm. Front row: Sam Byfield, Arnold Robson, Ronnie Lowen, Frank Hunter, John Warren, Derek Craig, W. Shield, Bob Irvin, Dave Hope, J. White, Eric Donnelly. Percy Brown, now aged ninety-two, was president of Burnopfield Bowling Club for twenty-six years, between 1974 and 2000.

Dennis Smith, the Burnopfield Park keeper, beside the floral display, which he used to commemorate the anniversaries of various local and national organizations over the years.

Looking from the plantation across Burnopfield Park with the Derwent Pavilion in the background, *c.* 1940. Entertainment in the village used to be provided by two picture halls. One was the Derwent Pavilion cinema, constructed around 1911, which was a rather ugly corrugated iron structure. It was located behind the old Brewery Yard on a site where the houses at 10-15 Willow View now stand.

Three ladies strolling along West View with the Derwent Pavilion Cinema behind them to the left, *c.* 1930.

The interior of the Derwent Pavilion, *c*. 1930. The Pavilion closed for films in around 1940 but continued as a dance hall and was used by Burnopfield Amateur Operatic and Dramatic Society (formed in 1939) for staging some of its shows. It eventually became derelict and was badly damaged in a storm in the 1960s before it was pulled down.

A Burnopfield Amateur Operatic and Dramatic Society production of *The Pirates of Penzance*, 1949. The Society gave shows at various venues in the area, including the Wesley Hall. This one was staged at Marley Hill Hall.

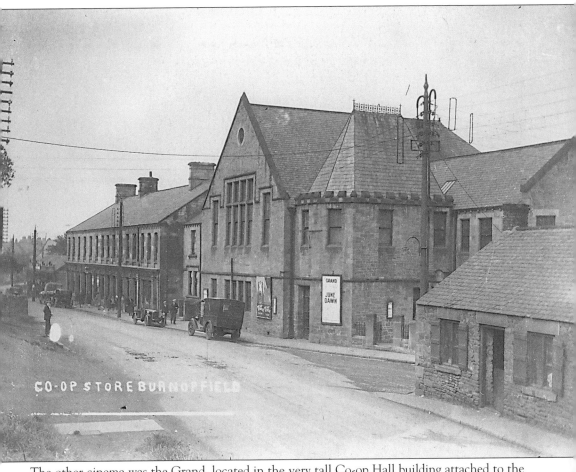

CO-OP STORE BURNOPFIELD

The other cinema was the Grand, located in the very tall Co-op Hall building attached to the old Burnopfield Co-operative Society buildings. It is seen here in around 1930, advertising the film *June Dawn*. The Co-op Hall was originally built in 1893 and part of it was leased as a cinema in 1912. It also contained a billiard room and a hall for meetings and functions. The billiard room was a dark, smoky place that was the venue for many a misspent youth!

Ivy Trotter, who was later to be awarded a British Empire Medal for her work in British intelligence during the Mau-Mau terrorist troubles in East Africa, used to play the piano in the Grand during the days of the silent movies. Mattie Baker, who was a familiar figure with his torch trying to keep the peace during performances, managed the Grand for more than twenty years together with his wife Doris who sold the tickets and the ice creams. The cheaper seats at the front were known as the 'dog end' and the seats at the back were usually occupied by courting couples. There was also an upstairs section. Normally considered to be the 'posh end', this became particularly lively during the Saturday morning matinées when the showing of swashbuckling epics such as *Zorro* and *The Man in the Iron Mask* would result in mass audience participation. The Grand eventually closed in 1960. The last show was an Elvis Presley film. It was converted into a restaurant, La Flambée, in the 1980s but this venture did not last long. The building became derelict and something of an eyesore in the village; for many years half of its roof was missing. Thankfully, this has now been restored and the building is in the process of being redeveloped.

Tommy Hudspith, 10 February 1954. He ran a wonderful old-fashioned confectionery shop on Front Street, just along from the Grand. The adventure of a Saturday morning matinée at the Grand was not complete without a visit to Tommy's magical shop on the way home, where wonderful jars of sweets and Frigidaires of juicy ice-lollies awaited any remaining pocket money.

Burnopfield Cricket Club, c. 1900, with Hares Drift at Dyke Heads in the background. Burnopfield Park had not yet been built. For more than 120 years, cricket has flourished in the village. There are two long-established teams at Burnopfield and Lintz and local rivalry is strong. It is difficult to say when Burnopfield Cricket Club began. The present cricket ground does not appear on the 1896 Ordnance Survey map, but does appear on the map published in 1921. However, records show that games were played before 1880.

Burnopfield Cricket Club, *c.* 1907, showing Cricket Terrace in the background. The houses on Lilac Crescent had not yet been built. The club has had the honour of producing two Test cricketers: Jim McConnon, who played for Glamorgan and England, and Colin Milburn, the 'Burnopfield Basher', who played for Northampton and England.

Burnopfield cricket team, before-1900.

The Burnopfield ladies' cricket team, *c.* 1947. From left to right, back row: Jenny Nevin, Betty Nevin, -?-, Mary McConnon, Bertha Milburn, Helen Tully, Mrs Lowes. Middle row: Jenny Potts, Verna Parker, Edna Brown, Jean Spoors, Lilian Uren, Helen Moody, Lily Brown, Lily Hall. Front row: -?-, -?-, Molly McTaff, -?-, -?-, -?-.

Jim McConnon (second right) on the MCC tour of Australia in 1954. Later that year, he played for England against Pakistan in the Third Test at Old Trafford and the Fourth Test at the Oval, where he broke a finger. A right-arm off-break bowler, Jim took four Test wickets. He was born on 21 June 1922 at Hawthorne Villa beside Cricket Terrace. He played only a few games for Burnopfield but his brothers Frank and Terry were regular members of the Burnopfield team. Jim's first-class career was spent with Glamorgan between 1950 and 1961, during which he took 799 wickets and scored 4,514 runs including 13 fifties. He now lives in retirement in Cheshire with his wife Pauline.

Colin Milburn in typical attacking mood playing for England against India in the Test Match at Edgbaston in 1967. Born on 23 October 1941, he played for England nine times, scoring 654 runs at an average of 46.71, including 2 centuries and 2 fifties. Tragically, on the evening of Friday 23 May 1969, at the age of twenty-seven, he lost his left eye in a car crash and never played for England again. Ironically, during the previous England winter tour of Pakistan, he had achieved his highest Test score of 139 in Karachi and seemed to have finally secured a regular Test place.

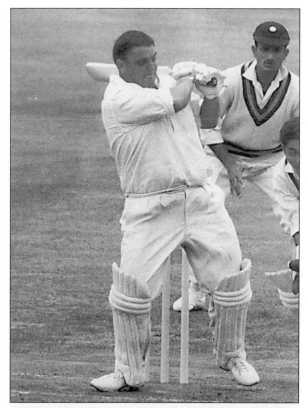

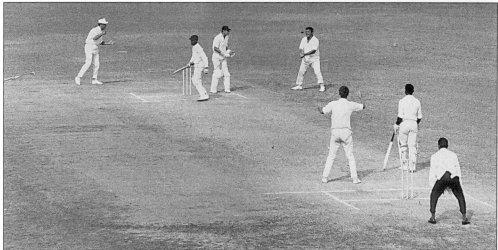

Colin Milburn taking a catch at Edgbaston for England against India in 1967 off the bowling of Derek Underwood, with Colin Cowdrey at first slip and Jim Parks keeping wicket. Milburn was an excellent short leg fielder; many of his 224 first-class catches were taken in this position. Colin played the majority of his first-class cricket for Northamptonshire but also had two seasons with Western Australia for whom he achieved his highest first-class score of 243 when playing against Queensland in Brisbane in 1968/69. Altogether he scored 13,262 runs in first-class cricket including 23 centuries and 75 fifties. Colin was also a useful medium-pace bowler, taking 99 first-class wickets.

Colin Milburn being presented to the Duke of Edinburgh during the Test match at Lords against Australia in 1968. As a boy, Colin dominated junior league cricket. His first ever senior match was in the Tyneside Senior League for Burnopfield Second XI at Greenside on 24 July 1954 when he scored 14 not out batting at number nine. He was then twelve years old. His second Tyneside Senior League game was on 28 August 1954 for Burnopfield First XI at South Moor when he scored a duck batting at number eleven. He eventually had 77 innings for Burnopfield First XI, scoring 1,985 runs at an average of 28.4, including 2 centuries and 10 fifties, and taking 105 wickets at an average of 16.3, all achieved before the age of eighteen. In 1959, Colin left Burnopfield to play for Chester-le-Street in the Durham Senior League and at the end of the season joined Northamptonshire who secured his services despite strong competition from Warwickshire. After his retirement from cricket, Colin had a successful career as a cricket commentator as well as taking part in many charity cricket matches all over the world. Tragically, on Wednesday 28 February 1990, at the age of forty-eight, Colin died exactly five years to the day after his father Jack, an equally powerful batsman, had died, and England lost a cricketing legend. Colin's funeral was held at Burnopfield Methodist church on Monday 5 March 1990 with Ian Botham and Mike Summerbee as two of the coffin bearers. His funeral was the biggest ever seen in Burnopfield, being attended by cricketers from local to Test level, as well as his many friends. Over 500 mourners crammed into the church to say goodbye to him in the presence of his mother, Bertha.

Bill Hewison (right), who used to play football for Sunderland. He signed for them in 1938 and played in the wartime leagues with the likes of Raich Carter. Bill was in the Sunderland team that won the wartime FA Cup final against Wolverhampton Wanderers. It was played over two legs. Sunderland won 4-1 at Wolves and the match at Roker was a 1-1 draw, before a crowd of 60,000. He eventually left Sunderland to play for Consett where he was rewarded with a pay rise: £4 per game compared to the £1 10s per week he had received at Sunderland! Locally, football has had a relatively low profile in Burnopfield. There are a number of pub and club teams who play in Saturday and Sunday leagues, but no one team has had a very long existence.

Dr Thomas Miller (left) being presented with a gift from the village by Jack Uren (right) on the occasion of his retirement as one of the village doctors in 1978. He had his surgery at No. 7 Grove Terrace for over forty years and he was famous for his cure-all yellow ointment. An avid collector of antiques, his surgery was full of paintings, statues and other objets d'art, as well as the sound of classical music provided by the BBC's Third Programme, as it was then.

An aerial photograph of part of Burnopfield from around 1993, showing the plantation, the cricket field and Lilac Crescent, which was built in 1936. After the Second World War, Stanley Urban District Council planted 48,000 trees on the slopes above Burnopfield from Syke Bank to Dyke Heads. This planting covered the scars of the open cast mining operations that had taken place on the bank top as well as depressions caused by mining subsidence. The trees are now well established and add to the beauty of the village.

The area where Lilac Crescent now stands, c. 1930. There used to be pigeon crees and allotments in the area before the new development.

Three

Place Names

How did Burnopfield get its name? One theory is that it is a combination of Saxon and Scandinavian words: 'burn' – a Saxon word for a small stream; 'hope' – a Scandinavian word shortened to 'op', meaning the head of a dene; and 'field' – from the Saxon word 'feld' meaning a fell or moor. Burnopfield is, therefore, 'the fell at the head of a dene with a stream running through'. This definition is certainly possible since there is a stream, which rises on the sloping hillside below Hobson and eventually makes its way into the dene near Bryan's Leap. This is further confirmed by the fact that there used to be three old red-tiled cottages called Dyke Heads (the head of a dyke or burn) between where Lilac Crescent now stands and the old Hobson Colliery. However, this theory is rather dull, a much more appealing alternative is as follows. In August 1640, a band of marauding Scots arrived on the north bank of the Tyne and pitched camp at Newburn. Having failed to capture Newcastle from the north, they decided to cross the Tyne and try from the south. The English anticipated this and sent a small detachment of troops to Stellahaugh where they quickly built some defensive earthworks. A Scottish officer frequently rode down to the river to refresh his horse, annoying an English officer so much that he fired at him and this shot started a battle. The small English force, being heavily outnumbered by the Scots, beat a hasty retreat. Many fled by way of Whickham, but others ran along the Derwent valley, up the hillside through Bryan's Leap, passing the little hamlet on the ridge of the hill with its fields of ripening corn. Here the order was given to set fire to the crops so that the fleeing English soldiers could make their escape under cover of smoke. After this, the little red-tiled hamlet became known as 'Burn-up-field'! Far-fetched, perhaps, but more romantic! Another possibility is the fact that as long ago as 1608, the area in which Burnopfield lies used to be called Bennetfield, which over the years may have been corrupted to Burnopfield. Maybe a simpler explanation is that someone of the name 'Burnop' or 'Burnip' owned a field where the village is now. We shall never know.

Bryan's Leap, Busty Bank, The Fold and Sheephill – just some of the odd place names with which Burnopfield is sprinkled.

Gibside from Bryan's Leap, 2000. There are several theories about the origin of the name 'Bryan's Leap'. The most obvious is that someone of that name made a prodigious leap on foot or on horseback over one of the nearby denes. However, why, when or with what result the leap was made is not known, although it must have been quite a leap to have been immortalized in the name of the place where it occurred. Another is that it may be a corruption of 'Bruin's Leap'. Many years ago bear-baiting was a common practice and maybe a bear, being baited in the village, leapt into the dene to escape. Interestingly, in parish records before 1871, the village of Burnopfield is often referred to as the 'Leap', the 'Loup', the 'Lop' or the 'Lope'. The nearby Leap Mill farm may have some connection with Bryan's Leap.

Leap Mill Farm, *c.* 1907. Thomas Linn built a watermill here over 250 years ago but over the years the site appears to have been used for several purposes. On the Ordnance Survey map published in 1862, the area around the modern day farm is described as 'The Leap Mills (Naphtha Manufactory)'. Naphtha and charcoal were manufactured in buildings near the mill. The same map also shows quarries on Busty Bank and between Burnopfield House and Sheephill. Work on restoring the mill began in 1988, and a replacement waterwheel was added during 1990 and 1991. The eighteenth-century Leap Mill Farm is now a Grade II listed building.

One of the old houses that used to be in the Fold, *c.* 1900. Next to Bryan's Leap is the area known as the Fold or, as it is sometimes still called in local dialect, the 'Faad'. This name probably arose from the fact that it was a place used for stabling horses used on the waggonways.

The original entrance to Sandypath Lane, 2000. Before the modern Bryan's Leap housing estate was built, Sandypath Lane (or the Sandy Lonnen as it is known locally) used to run uninterrupted from the main road. It started opposite the Brewery Yard, passing what used to be Bryan's Leap Farm on its left and the old Flower Show field on its right, before winding its way over the fields to join up with the Burnopfield to Rowlands Gill road. Although part of it had to be diverted to accommodate the housing estate, panoramic views of the Derwent Valley can still be seen from the fields on either side of the lane.

Gibside from the south, by J.M.W. Turner, 1815. If you had walked up Sandypath Lane in 1815, you might have seen the lone figure of a man standing in one of these fields with an artist's easel in front of him. This artist was none other than the famous landscape painter who had been commissioned by the Strathmores to paint a picture of the Gibside Estate. The painting shows Gibside Hall, the Monument, the Chapel and the tree-lined Avenue. It hung for many years in the Tate Art Gallery in London.

Sheephill from the Sandypath Lane area, *c.* 1950. It is easy to understand how Sheephill got its name, but nearby there used to be a place marked on old maps as 'Sparrow Hall'. A story is told that a doctor who lived in the vicinity in the 1960s received a letter addressed to the 'Squire of Sparrow Hall'; it made his day!

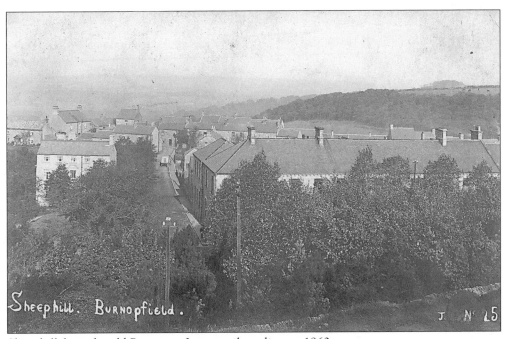

Sheephill from the old Pontop to Jarrow railway line, *c.* 1960.

Busty Bank, *c*. 1900. The name 'Busty Bank' is probably derived from a steep bank on the Gibside Estate through which a road had been cut, exposing a seam of coal. Under the action of frost and rain, the bank began to crumble onto the road. This hilly road became known as 'Bursting Bank', then 'Bursty Bank' and finally Busty Bank. The exposed seam of coal was named the 'Busty' and was first worked at the spot where it had been discovered, for the use of the owners of Gibside and the tenants. It continued to be worked from this spot until an accident occurred, which killed at least one and possibly several of the miners. Not far from this spot, the Busty Seam was found to have a band of stone it, which increased in thickness to the north and west to such an extent that it could no longer be worked as one seam. Instead it had to be worked as two seams, known locally as the 'Top Busty' and the 'Bottom Busty'. The Busty Seam extended over a very large area and was extremely important to the development of Burnopfield and the surrounding villages. Eventually, it was worked in most of the pits in the northern part of County Durham.

Four

Burnopfield House

William Newton, one of three brothers from a wealthy coal owning family, built Burnopfield House in the 1720s. The Newtons came to Burnopfield from their family residence at Cold Pike Hall in Lanchester. They were evidently very successful in the coal trade; this was confirmed by an entry in the Gentlemen's Magazine published in London on 28 August 1749. This announced that a Government grant had been awarded to Mr William Newton of Burnopfield and Mr Thomas Stokoe of Bryan's Leap, both gentlemen of great experience in the coal trade, for a newly invented method of drawing coals, stones etc. out of deep pits or mines. William Newton died on 21 November 1763, aged sixty-three years. Shortly afterwards, scandal came to the Newton family when Hannah Newton, William's daughter and heiress to the family fortune of £20,000 per annum, met an Irish adventurer, Lt Andrew Robinson Stoney. Aware of her wealth, Stoney married her in 1766 and they went to live at Cold Pike Hall. There, his ill treatment of her became a local scandal, and within a few years she and her child died and were buried at Tanfield.

From about 1825 to 1925, the Watson family lived at Burnopfield House. They were a family who produced a number of eminent doctors including John Watson (1790-1847), a surgeon who set up a medical practice in the village, and later his son Henry William Watson (1821-1886) who took over the practice. Dr Robert Stirling, who was brutally murdered at midday on 1 November 1855 in Smailes Lane, Rowlands Gill (see also p. 2), assisted Henry William Watson for a tragically short period. So did Dr John Snow (1813-1858) who later became a famous epidemiologist and anaesthetist. Mary Watson, the widow of Henry William Watson, and her family continued to live at Burnopfield House after his death. Mary died in 1917 at Selkirk in Scotland, where she had gone in the hope of improving her failing health. She was buried in St James' churchyard alongside her husband. After the Watson family moved out in 1925, John Charlton set up a sawmill business on the estate. Later, Norman Hall bought Burnopfield House. He repaired its façade and added a wing for use as his haulage company's offices. Subsequent attempts to turn Burnopfield House into a luxury pub run by Nimmo's were unsuccessful and it was converted into three residential apartments for which it is still used today.

The impressive façade of Burnopfield House, 2000.

The original entrance to Burnopfield House is on the left of this photograph taken in around 1910.

The Coachman's House at Burnopfield House, *c.* 1910.

A caricature of Stoney Bowes, who was used by the writer Thackeray as a model for his reprobate character Barry Lyndon. Stoney was an out-and-out rogue who possessed charm and wit but who could be unspeakably cruel. Having mistreated his first wife and child to such an extent that they both died, he set off for London with his wife's fortune of £20,000 per year. Here he met the fabulously wealthy widowed Mary Eleanor Bowes, Countess of Strathmore, who owned the Gibside Estate. Stoney eventually tricked her into marriage in 1777, and having to adopt her family name of Bowes, he became the notorious Stoney Bowes. Her subsequent miserable life with him became one of the biggest scandals of the period. Fortunately, however, she had protected her fortune of over £1 million by secretly drawing up an ante-nuptial trust. As a result, he ended up in poverty and his predicament is said to have given rise to the expression 'Stoney Broke'. The full story can be found in Ralph Arnold's book *The Unhappy Countess*.

Dr Henry Watson (seated) and his family in the grounds of Burnopfield House, *c.* 1880.

Smailes Lane and Stirling Lane signs, Rowlands Gill. In 1855, Dr Henry Watson advertised for a locum to help him with his extensive practice, which covered both sides of the Derwent Valley. A young Scottish doctor, Robert Stirling, aged twenty-five, applied and was accepted for the post. Dr Stirling had already applied to be a surgeon in the British Army, then fighting in the Crimea. His intention was to stay in Burnopfield until he received his calling-up papers.

Mr John Edward Iley, a Burnopfield co-operative greengrocer, pictured near the old railway arch at the bottom of Stirling Lane, Rowlands Gill, *c. 1930*. Doctor Stirling, after whom the lane is named, had only been in Burnopfield for about ten days when on 1 November 1855 he set off to visit patients at Thornley and the Spen. He was last seen alive at 1 p.m. on his way back to Burnopfield by a farmer who had exchanged greetings with him in Smailes Lane at the bottom of Rowlands Gill bank. The same farmer had earlier passed two men whose appearance he had not liked. A short time after meeting Dr Stirling, the farmer heard a shot. When Dr Stirling didn't turn up in Burnopfield, Dr Watson assumed that he had received his calling-up papers and had left to join the Army. However, his mother, in Kirkintilloch in Scotland, had a premonition that something had happened and his parents rushed to Burnopfield. Search parties were sent out and on 6 November his body was found near the railway bridge, which used to stand at the end of Smailes Lane, Rowlands Gill. The bridge was always referred to after that as 'Doctor's Murder Bridge', and the area was said to be haunted for some years afterwards. He had been shot and severely battered over the head with the butt of a gun. His throat had been cut and his body dragged through a fence and dumped in some bushes. His silver watch, ring, money and lancets had been stolen. Interestingly, about forty years ago, a watch bearing the initials R.S. and matching exactly the description of the one stolen from Dr Stirling was left to Dr Stephen Boland of Burnopfield in the will of one of his elderly women patients.

The former Smailes Lane, Rowlands Gill, 2000. It was widely believed that Doctor Stirling had been mistaken for Mr John Errington, landlord of the Bute Arms at High Spen. Mr Errington had been expected to pass down Smailes Lane that afternoon on his way to Gibside Hall to pay his rent to his landlord Mr John Bowes. It was said that Mr Errington strongly resembled the doctor in appearance. For months afterwards, he suffered from shock, refusing to venture out-of-doors, and he eventually died at a comparatively early age.

Dr Stirling's tombstone in Tanfield churchyard. In March 1856, two men were arrested and charged with the murder, they were John Cain (also known as 'Whisky' Jack because of the illicit still he ran near Smailes Lane at the time of the murder) and Richard Rayne, who had a blacksmith's forge in Winlaton. Oddly, before the trial, Dr Stirling's mother identified Cain as the man she had seen murder her son in her dream. However, the evidence was purely circumstantial and Cain and Rayne were acquitted. Part of Smailes Lane was renamed Stirling Lane in memory of the young doctor and serves as a constant reminder of his tragic story today.

Five

The Leazes

Travelling west from Bryan's Leap along the present-day main road brings you to The Leazes. Originally, this area formed part of a moor known as Bartram Leazes or Leazes Common, which was later exploited during the coal years by the opening up of a number of mines in the area. The earliest Ordnance Survey map of 1856 shows only a few buildings in the Leazes area, a farm, a hall and a few houses. Nowadays, both sides of the main road are built up. The left-hand side of the road includes Burnopfield Junior School, the Gospel Fellowship church, The Temperance Hall and the Travellers' Rest public house, as well as residential houses. The Travellers' Rest is still referred to locally as 'Jack Allan's' after a former landlord who used to play centre forward for Newcastle United during the 1930s. The right-hand side consists mainly of residential houses but at the far end, behind a large stone wall on the opposite side of the road to St James's church and next to the old vicarage, is Leazes Hall, the oldest house in The Leazes.

St James's church, the parish church of Burnopfield, was completed in 1873. At the time of its construction, the site on which it stands was reported in the press as being 'behind a picturesque cluster of trees, immediately over the brow of a hill in the valley of the Derwent and commanding one of the most extensive panoramas of landscape to be found in the North of England'. In about 1930, St James's church almost fell down due to subsidence caused by colliery workings. The bell turret apparently leaned at an angle of 45 degrees and to this day there are no walls absolutely perpendicular and no angles of 90 degrees.

The main road continues on past the church towards High Friarside and eventually on to join the Shotley Bridge road at the bottom of Medomsley Bank. Outside the main entrance to St James's church, the road from Pickering Nook forms a junction with the Shotley Bridge Road and both sides of this road are now also built up as far as the bottom of the Syke Bank. The buildings here are mainly residential but there is also Burnopfield Youth and Community Centre (formerly the Leazes School), a newsagent's shop, a post office and a grocery shop. All these have been added in the relatively recent past. The same Ordnance Survey map referred to earlier shows no buildings at all next to this road.

Burnopfield Secondary Modern School viewed from the plantation above Burnopfield park, *c.* 1950. In 1968, this became Burnopfield Junior and Infants' School.

The Leazes seen from St James's church along the main road, *c.* 1920.

Leazes School (now Burnopfield Youth and Community Centre), *c.* 1905. This continued as a school until 1968 when the children were moved to the old secondary modern school building. After some negotiation, the Burnopfield Community Association, which had been formed in 1966, was given permission to use these premises and the Burnopfield Community Centre became a reality. It celebrated its Silver Jubilee in 1993 and is still going strong.

Leazes viewed from the top of Syke Bank, *c.* 1910, with St James's church on the horizon on the left. There used to be a kippering factory at the bottom of Syke Bank kept by George Rowley. The detached house in the centre burnt down in 1947 and an occupant by the name of Mickey Rooney died in the fire.

Leazes Hall, 1876. Sometimes called Leazes House, this was the family seat for the Leazes estate, which was formed out of a portion of the confiscated de Linz estate, which included High Friarside. In 1711, the heiress to this portion, Jane Hancock, married a William Scaife, gentleman of the Leazes, after whom the nearby Scaife's Wood is named. The Scaifes are believed to have built Leazes Hall as a family residence about this time. At some time during the nineteenth century, it is said that the hall was used as a boarding school for girls.

Leazes Hall, c. 1940. In 1888 Leazes Hall was transferred to the South Garesfield Coal Company, and was then occupied by its agent, Colonel Shiel, and his wife and family. They took a very active part in village life, organizing pageants and other events in the Hall grounds. During the First World War, Colonel Shiel helped to recruit many soldiers from the local mines. In both world wars, it was used as a meeting place for the Territorials and the Home Guard. After the nationalization of the coal industry, the National Coal Board took over Leazes Hall and its agent, Colonel Kirkup, lived there, and Queen Elizabeth (now the Queen Mother) visited him on at least one occasion. It now serves as a private residential and nursing home.

A Burnopfield Amateur Operatic and Dramatic Society production of *Robin of Sherwood*, 1939. At the beginning of the Second World War, with the help of Mrs Shiel, the Burnopfield Amateur Operatic and Dramatic Society was formed to help raise money for the Spitfire Fund.

The Revd Thomas Stirrup, who in 1868 was appointed by the Parish of St Margaret's Tanfield to look after Burnopfield and Lintz Colliery. When the new Parish of Burnopfield came into being in 1871, he became the first vicar of Burnopfield. He held regular Sunday morning services in a schoolroom at Lintz Colliery where he initially had nine communicants and a choir of two. Curiously, the Offertory Book for 1871 states that 2,008 coins were given in the morning collections and 1,345 in the evening collections. Revd Stirrup left Burnopfield for Barrow-in-Furness in 1891, where he exchanged livings with the Revd G.T. Dunne. Ironically, both were in ill health and both were seeking less laborious fields.

St James's church, c. 1880. The new parish of Burnopfield took in part of Crookgate, Crookbank, Hobson, Burnopfield, Lintz, North Lintz and Ewehurst Head. The population of the parish in 1872 was estimated to be 2,900; by 1891 it had risen to about 4,100. Because of increasing attendance at the services, it became apparent that a parish church must be built. Thanks largely to the efforts of Revd Stirrup, Mr Richard Hodgson Huntley, a local landowner, gave a site at the Leazes on which to build a church, with sufficient space for a churchyard around it. A Church Building Fund was started, and on 21 May 1872 Lord Ravensworth laid the foundation stone of the new church. The stone contained a cavity in which was placed a large bottle containing newspapers and coins of the period, and a Latin inscription. By the autumn of 1873, the church had been completed and the churchyard had been walled. Some 80ft long and 40ft wide, the church was built of stone in the Early English style at a cost of £2,500 and could accommodate about 320 people. The Lord Bishop of Durham, the Revd Charles Baring, consecrated the church on 20 November 1873. The Revd Stirrup took the first service on Sunday 23 November 1873 when there were twenty-five communicants present.

The interior of St James's church, 1873. It consists of a nave with a south aisle, a chancel and an organ chamber on the south, and a vestry on the north. There is a turreted belfry at the east end of the nave. The aisle is divided from the nave by an arcade of four pointed arches supported on cylindrical pillars.

The former vicarage, 1990. Between 1876 and 1877 the Revd Stirrup succeeded in having a vicarage built on the opposite side of the road to the church after having to fight hard to obtain some money from the Ecclesiastical Commission.

The 1st Burnopfield Scout Troop, c. 1932, with their scoutmaster, Mr Hughes. This was formed during the incumbency of the Reverend Brigstock (1931-1933). In February 1986, Noble Parker was given a surprise party at St James's church hall to celebrate his fifty years in the Scout movement. He joined the 1st Burnopfield Troop at the age of eleven and in 1953 he set up the 2nd Burnopfield Scout Troop. Noble is now the president of Burnopfield Cricket Club.

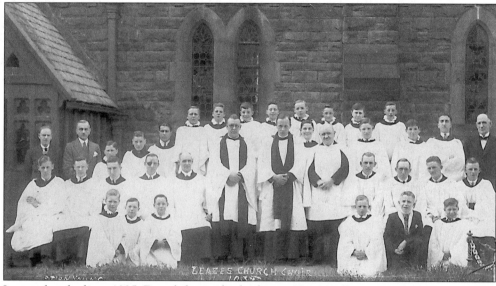

Leazes church choir, 1935. From left to right, back row: Harry Milburn, George Layton, Robert Middleton, Joe Oliphant, William Lennox, Marvyn Long, Fred Carr, Harry Williams. Second row (standing): J. Cunningham (sexton), Frank Braidford (churchwarden), Robert Johnson (boy), Earnest Hope (alto), Harry Minto (bass), Revd James (curate), Revd A.J. Heaver (vicar), Norman Batey (boy), Mr W.C. Davis (organist and choirmaster), Robert Dent (boy), Noble Parker (boy), Dick Carr (alto), Mr Albert Patterson (churchwarden). Second row (sitting): William Stones (alto), Jack Patterson (alto), Robert Carr (bass), William Turnbull (tenor), George Kirby (tenor), Joe Middleton (tenor), Arnold Parker (bass), Douglas Cheeseman (bass), Alan Cheeseman (tenor). Front row (kneeling): Stanley Hope, Walter Oliphant, Jack Adamson, Alex Nevin, Jack Cunningham (organ blower), Enoch Layton.

74

St James's church hall, 2000. Also shown to the left is Twin Gables, one of the oldest surviving houses in the Leazes, built in 1828. During the second half of the nineteenth century, in the reign of Queen Victoria, drinking and drunkenness were very prevalent throughout the country. As a result of this, several Temperance Movements were formed, and people, especially the young, were encouraged to join. The Sons of Temperance societies became very strong and, in most villages and towns, rooms were hired where meetings were held, and discussions took place on the evils of over-indulgence in alcohol. Just such a Temperance Movement started in the little hamlet of Lintzford, situated on the River Derwent, 2 or 3 miles from Burnopfield. This became known as the Lintzford Band of Hope. Very little is known of its development, but the members must have been ardent workers because, in 1872, they built a Temperance Hall at Leazes, Burnopfield, for their meetings to be held. Because of subsidence caused by coal workings, it collapsed on two occasions and needed extensive repairs. It was eventually purchased by a Miss Allgood and presented to the church for the use of parishioners. Since then to the present day, St James's church hall, as it is now called, has been a focal point of church social activities. Concerts, plays, dances, sport in the form of badminton, billiards and table tennis, Scout troops, Cubs, Girl Guides, Brownies, play groups and toddler groups have all taken part in the programme of events.

Inspired by the need to worship in an 'evangelical' church, Reuben Dews and the lady who was later to become his wife, Florrie Stobbs, together with many local volunteers, erected the first Gospel Fellowship church in Burnopfield in 1948. It was a humble building, made from compressed cardboard covered with felt and bitumen and having a corrugated iron roof. The first convert was a local drunkard, Geordie Morton, who became a reformed character and the first caretaker of the church, being famed for his immaculate gardens.

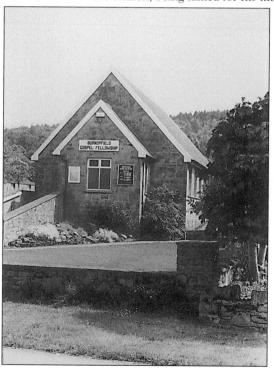

Due to the success of the fellowship, a larger building was soon required. In 1956, the land and buildings of the old Constitution Club between the original church and the Burnopfield Modern School were purchased and, on Saturday 27 October 1962, after considerable voluntary efforts, a new church was opened, exactly fourteen years to the day after the opening of the first. By 1976, a fibreglass baptistry had been installed and the first baptism was performed in it in April 1977.

Six

Lintz

Half a mile or so to the west of the Leazes is the village of Lintz, a name that has been associated with this area for hundreds of years. The spelling of Lintz has changed many times over the centuries with variations such as Lynce, Lynths, Lynz and Lynze all being recorded at one time or another. The name itself is derived from that of a wealthy family, known as 'de Lynz', who settled in the area before or during the twelfth century. Probably originating from the area near the modern city of Linz in Austria, it is believed that they moved to England to escape religious persecution. Granted to them by the Norman kings of England, the family estate was originally known as the Villa of Lynz, at the centre of which was a fine house, known as Lynz Hall. This was probably built early in the thirteenth century. The ground floor had six rooms; there were five rooms on the first floor, and an attic, which was used as a chapel by monks in the area. Because of their turbulent past, the family built a passage round the house between the inner and outer walls for use as a refuge in times of danger. They also built a small chapel in the nearby Priestfield area, similar to the one at Friarside. In 1352, the Bishop of Durham confiscated the estate from Richard de Lynz when his son, Thomas, was outlawed for felony. The estate changed hands several times over the centuries and was divided into portions. Lynz Hall was eventually converted into a farmhouse but this fell into ruins. These could still be seen at the beginning of the twentieth century, but they have now completely gone, the last stones being used to build batteries for egg production in a local chicken farm.

The rural calm of the Villa of Lynz was shattered in the year 1855 when a number of pits were opened in the area and the village of Lintz Colliery was created. The village thrived; soon it had its own public house, Methodist chapel, recreational facilities and Miners' Institute. However, when the colliery closed in 1929, the surface works were all cleared away, the shafts were filled up and the large pit spoil heaps were levelled. The old terraces were later demolished and replaced by a pleasant estate of brick-built houses with lawns and open grass spaces. Of the old village, only the public house remains. Today, there is practically nothing to show that mining flourished for almost a hundred years in this district, except the grass-grown sites of the old waggonways.

The Billy Pit, Lintz Colliery, c. 1900. There was another pit called the Anna Pit. The colliery was worked by Messrs McLean and Prior and continued until 1885, when it was laid in, causing considerable depression to the mining community at Lintz. In 1889, it was reopened by John Shield, Esq. and in 1894 it had an annual output of about 83,700 tons and gave employment to about 260 men and boys. It eventually closed in 1929; the coal still left being worked from South Garesfield Colliery at nearby Friarside, chiefly by the Lintz miners who were transferred there.

Lintz Colliery employees, 1881.

Number 33 School Street, Lintz, *c.* 1900. The old village of Lintz Colliery, consisted of long rows of primitive stone-built terraced houses with muck midden toilets outside. The houses were built with little thought for the comfort of the people who had to occupy them, the dominant factor being to economise as much as possible on space, labour and materials. The typical cost of building each one was about £40.

The Albion Inn, *c.* 1950. It was originally owned by Mr John Nevin and was built around 1898. At first it was called Albion House and part of it was a grocer's shop.

The Lintz Miners' Institute, which was formed from the old Lintz School building, seen here in around 1920. The 'Tute', as it was affectionately called, had several billiard tables. Money was hard to come by to pay for the games, so youths went around the village shovelling miners' coals into their coalhouses for sixpence a load. Billiards tournaments among the surrounding villages were a feature between the wars, and there were many excellent players. Snooker was less common then than it is today, but the institute boasted a ladies' English snooker champion, Ruth Harrison.

The Lintz Methodist church, seen here around 1910, opened on 10 February 1903. Thomas Oakley is second from the left, George Cromarty is first on the right and Edward Cushing is second from the right. Before 1903, the Lintz Methodist Society, which had been in existence for many years, had met in the homes of its members and probably also in Lintz Colliery School after it was built in 1863. The last service was held in the church on Sunday 25 November 1962 and its various artefacts were distributed to other Methodist churches in the area. The church building was eventually razed to the ground and some of its stones were incorporated in a bungalow built on its old site.

The interior of the Lintz Methodist church during a harvest festival, *c.* 1910. It is certainly before the organ was fitted in 1926.

Lintz Wesleyan Women's Own, 1932.

Lintz Cricket Club, with William Street in the background, c. 1910. Formed about 1905, Lintz still has a thriving cricket club. Its most famous victory, however, was not on the pitch but in the Court of Appeal. In 1971 new houses were built on a green-field site next to the ground and, in 1972, a Mr and Mrs Miller moved into one of them. They were soon in a bitter dispute with the club due to balls landing on their garden and roof. In 1976, in the High Court case of Miller v. Jackson and Others (Bob Jackson was the club's chairman) cricket was banned until balls could be prevented from being struck out of the ground. Since this was impossible, the ground was faced with closure. The club appealed and, to the relief of similar clubs all over the country, the injunction was lifted by a majority of two to one.

Lintz from the air in 1984, showing the cricket field and the adjoining football field. The Millers' house was the last semi-detached on the left along the top edge of the ground. They considered appealing to the House of Lords but eventually moved away in 1978.

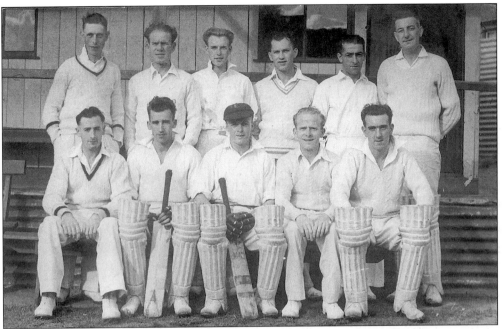

Lintz cricket team, 1954. From left to right, back row: Billy Cushing, Billy Cunningham, A. Rix, Ernie Wintrip, Jack Nevin, Bill Carradice. Front row: Bill Barnes, Bobby Moore, John Cromarty, Jack Cunningham, Bobby Cromarty. Interestingly, three well-known footballers in the North East have played cricket for Lintz. These were: Frank Clark (Newcastle United and later manager of Nottingham Forest), David Elliott (Sunderland) and Frank Spraggon (Middlesbrough).

Lintz ladies' football team, 1926. From left to right, back row: Evelyn Aspinall, E. Booth, E. O'Neill, N. Booth, A. Hickman, J. Reay, E. Pyle, -?-. Front row: Rosie Convery, Annie Pyle, Mary Nevin, Maggie Dunn, Katie Neasham. Teams from the Albion Inn and the Travellers' Rest have used the football field in recent years. In earlier days, both Lintz Celtic and Lintz Ladies had very successful football teams.

Priestfield Lodge, c. 1980. Slightly to the west of modern Lintz is the area known as Priestfield, where monks used to till the fields, hence the name. The main house in this area is Priestfield Lodge, possibly built around 1870 on the site of some earlier cottages. Priestfield used to be a stagecoach stop on the Newcastle to Shotley Bridge route. In earlier days, there used to be at least one and possibly two chapels in the nearby Lofthouse area where the monks who worked at Priestfield lived. Stones from one of these chapels were used in the construction of Priestfield Lodge.

Lintz Green House, 2000. To the west of Priestfield is Lintz Green, which was once considered to be a township in the ancient parish of Tanfield. It comprised Burnopfield, The Leazes, High Friarside and Priestfield. However, Lintz Green is now a very quiet and secluded spot although it does boast a very fine house, Lintz Green House, parts of which were also built using stones from one of the old chapels in the Lofthouse area. The present Lintz Green House built around 1826 as an extension of a property owned by a Mr Clowes. One of the rooms in Lintz Green House has always had extra-strong shutters at its windows. This is thought to have been the room of a 'mad' member of one of the previous families who lived there.

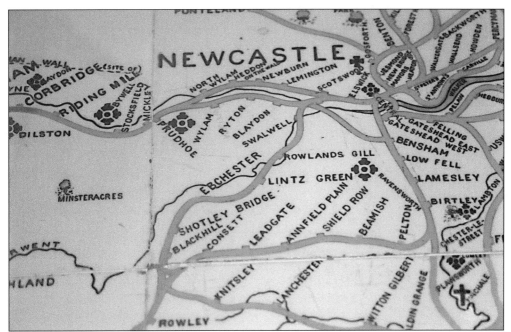

Map of old railways showing Lintz Green station. In 1867, when the Derwent Valley Branch Railway between Newcastle and Consett opened, Lintz Green was one of only two railway stations (the other being at Rowlands Gill) for miles around for anyone wishing to travel to Newcastle and beyond. Despite the long walks involved, both stations were very busy. It was at Lintz Green station that an infamous murder took place in 1911. The line was closed in 1954 and the tracks were taken up in 1964.

Lintz Green railway station, 1911. The building shown on the platform housed the first class waiting room (the bay window on the left) and the booking office (the bay window on the right). On the night of Saturday 7 October 1911, George Wilson, the stationmaster at Lintz Green, was waiting on the platform shown above with Fred White the booking clerk and John Routledge the porter for the arrival of the last train to Newcastle that night.

The down platform (on the left) and the up platform (right), 1911. The train pulled up at the down platform at 10.42 p.m. and four men got off. These were Samuel Elliott, Robert Wailes, Thomas Middleton and Charles Swinburne. Elliott, Wailes and Middleton crossed the line and set off on the footpath to their homes at Low Friarside about a mile away. Swinburne waited for Fred White to finish his work before accompanying him down the narrow lane to Lintzford. Having seen the train away, Wilson and White said goodnight to each other.

The stationmaster's house in 1911, showing George Wilson inset. George Wilson made his way to the stationmaster's house where he lived, about 50 yards away, while White locked the booking office. Just as he locked the door, he heard a shot coming from the direction of the stationmaster's house. He and Swinburne ran towards the house where they met Wilson's daughter, Bertha, and Elliott, Wailes and Middleton who had dashed back when they too had heard the shot. Middleton stumbled across the body of George Wilson beside the gate outside the house and he and Elliott carried him inside. Wilson was alive but covered in blood and unable to speak; within a few minutes he died.

Dr Wynne Boland with his sons Stephen and Harry. Doctor Boland and the police were called and a murder investigation began. The next morning the bullet was found along with a small bag containing sand and a linen cloth in the form of a gag. The motive for the murder was probably robbery. Normally, after the last train had gone to Newcastle, George Wilson carried the day's takings from the booking office to his house. Ironically, however, on the night he was killed, he had taken the money home an hour earlier, after the last train had gone through to Consett.

The inquest was held in the first class waiting room seen on the right above. Soon, over 200 policemen were involved in the murder hunt but they had little success, much to the annoyance of the local press. Suddenly, however, after forcing their way into his house in Byker and questioning him thoroughly, they arrested Samuel Atkinson, the relief porter at Lintz Green station, on suspicion of murder. Atkinson was brought to trial but the case against him was dismissed on a technicality. The police had forgotten to caution him during their initial questioning and the presiding judge ruled that everything he told them was inadmissible.

Witnesses and police officers waiting for the inquest to be held, 9 October 1911. Thomas Middleton is seen second from the right; his grandson Terry Middleton OBE is currently postmaster at Rowlands Gill post office. George Wilson was buried in St James's churchyard. Hundreds of people attended the funeral service, which was held outside his own front door, before following the cortège the three miles to the churchyard. Because of the intense local interest, a film of the funeral procession was later shown at the Derwent Pavilion cinema, which had then been open only a few weeks.

The stationmaster's house, 2000. Although the booking office and waiting room have long gone and the Derwent Walk has replaced the tracks, the stationmaster's house still remains. Now in private ownership, one of its previous occupants claimed some years ago that a bullet hole could once be plainly seen in the door. Rumours also persist that a train can be heard passing through the station at midnight on the anniversary of the murder and that George Wilson's ghost still haunts the place.

Viaduct over Fogoes Burn, *c*. 1900. Walking west along the Derwent Valley Walk from the site of Lintz Green station brings you to first to the viaduct over Fogoes Burn and then a few hundred yards later to the longer and equally elegant viaduct over the Pont Burn.

The Old Mill, Lintz Green.

The Old Mill, Lintz Green, *c*. 1910. Below the Pont Burn viaduct, beside the road bridge over the burn, there is now a parking area for cars. Here, there used to be a corn mill and a blacksmith's shop.

Lintzford village, 1913. From Lintz Green, a dirt lane runs past the Sliding Braes (so called because water springs cause the lane to slip) to Lintzford about half a mile away. Here there was once a ford across the River Derwent before the single span bridge was built, possibly in 1645. Lintzford now stands on the main road through the Derwent Valley from Rowlands Gill to Shotley Bridge. However, it is believed to lie on a pre-Roman footpath from Jarrow to Blanchland, which passed by Friarside Chapel. The terraces of twenty cottages, seen above, which were built in the nineteenth century for the paper mill workers, were demolished in 1966.

The old Lintzford mill buildings and chimney, c. 1980. As long ago as 1587, records show that there was a corn mill at Lintzford. In about 1695, it was turned into a paper mill, the rent being £7 per annum plus one sword blade well-made and tempered. It continued as such until 1922 being run for many years by the Annandale family, who also built the elegant Lintzford House in about 1790. In 1923, the mill was converted into Richardson's Printing Ink factory and in 1966 was taken over by a paint company. Finally, around 1990, the chimney was taken down and the buildings were converted into fine executive homes.

Seven

The Friarsides

If you walk along the footpath next to the main road between St James's church and the old vicarage with the church on your left, you pass a Victorian post box in the stone wall on your right before reaching the village graveyard on the side of the hill. A short distance further on, there is a road off to the right, which leads steeply down the hill towards the River Derwent. The area around the top of this road is known as High Friarside and was originally part of the Villa of Lynz, which belonged to the de Lynz family. Just to the west of St James's church, where there is now a modern housing estate, used to be High Friarside Farm.

Walking from High Friarside down the steep hill brings you first to Middle Friarside and then to Low Friarside, not far from the Derwent Walk, the former route of the old Consett to Newcastle railway line. There used to be villages at Middle and Low Friarside to service the nearby South Garesfield Colliery. Slightly to the east of Low Friarside is Jockside Burn, which flows through Jockside Wood. This burn runs under the Derwent Walk to Low Friarside Farm where, in a field just to the north, is the roofless ruin of Friarside chapel, one of the oldest buildings in the area. This is supposed to have been founded by a hermit named John or Johan about 1150, who would have been a friar or a brother. He had been looking for a suitable place to live in solitude for many years but had been turned away by all the landowners he had approached. Eventually, he enlisted the help of St Godric (1090-1170), a hermit who lived at Finchale. St Godric interceded on his behalf with Reginald, Bishop of Durham, who granted permission to John to look for a suitable location. When John returned to St Godric having found his ideal spot, he was amazed to hear him describe the site in minute detail despite the fact that St Godric had not left his cell for years. This spot was Friarside but the origin of its name is uncertain. One possibility is that it comes from a shortening of Friar-John-Side or Friar-Johan-Side; another is that it used to be called Frere-Host-Side which became corrupted first to Frere-Side and then Friarside. In living memory, the local name for Friarside was Jockside, a name still retained in nearby Jockside Wood and Jockside Burn. This may be a corruption of John Side or Johan Side in the local dialect.

In 1979, the historic Victorian post-box opposite St James's church was saved from demolition by the then vicar of Burnopfield, the Revd Noel Toogood. Derwentside District Council had given permission to have it removed after the Post Office had claimed it was letting in water. The Revd Toogood raised a petition, involved Radio 4 and managed to persuade the Post Office to carry out renovation work.

The old humpback bridge on the B6310 over the old Lintz Colliery waggonway to Low Friarside. The bridge was demolished in 1986 and now only traces of the waggonway remain.

The road junction at High Friarside, which leads to Middle Friarside and Low Friarside. In the foreground is the Garden of Remembrance at St James's church, which was opened in 1997.

An old street of houses, Nos 7-13 High Friarside, which was demolished in the 1940s.

A view dating from around 1910 of some of the twenty or so houses at Middle Friarside that were demolished in the 1930s, when it was razed to the ground. All that remains now are traces of an odd three-sided earthwork just to the east of the road. One suggestion is that this used to be a reservoir in which the monks from nearby Friarside Chapel stored their fish. Another is that it could have provided a moat for a manor house that has long since been demolished. Whatever it was, it was probably constructed before the dissolution of the monasteries in 1539-1540.

One of the wooden houses at Low Friarside, *c.* 1900, where there used to be thirty-three houses arranged as a terrace and a square, and also a children's playground. These and the houses at Middle Friarside provided homes for some of the miners and their families from nearby South Garesfield Colliery. In 1933, the houses at Low Friarside were condemned and demolished.

94

South Garesfield Colliery, Tilley Drift, 1902. A rope-operated railway line for coal trucks ran from Lintz Colliery to Low Friarside and then linked into the Consett to Newcastle railway line. In 1894, the colliery had an annual output of 80,000 tons of coal and provided work for about 230 men and boys.

The South Garesfield Colliery manager's house at Low Friarside, *c.* 1900. The manager was Mr Braidford.

South Garesfield Colliery staff and workmen, 1908.

All that remains of South Garesfield Colliery are a few of the old surface buildings and a number of small marker stones indicating the sites of the old pit shafts.

Friarside Chapel, 2000. In the *Bolden Book* of 1183, mention is made of a hermit living near the River Derwent. However, the earliest reference to the name Friarside in literature, in the form of 'Frere Johanside nigh Derwent', is in Bishop Kelland's register of 1312. The ruins take the form of a rectangular building some 49ft by 20ft, the eastern part of which is a chapel and the western part the dwelling place of the friar, the latter being much less ornate than the former. The east gable is almost intact and the remains of the tracery of the windows indicate fourteenth century Decorated work. The walls are about $2\frac{1}{2}$ft thick. It is an example of one of the many monastic cells or hospitals of the Middle Ages. The chapel was dedicated to St Mary the Virgin. The duties of the friar were to perform the rites of the Church for the foresters and labourers who formed the sparse population in the area, and to give hospitality to passing travellers. It has been suggested that Friarside lay on a pilgrims' footpath from Jarrow to Blanchland and that pilgrims may have rested there before continuing their journey. After the Dissolution of the Monasteries in about 1539, the last chaplain was pensioned off at £5 per annum for the remainder of his life, the bell at the east end was taken away, and the building was confiscated by the Crown. In 1592, Queen Elizabeth I granted it to Thomas Liddell of Ravensworth who, in turn, granted it to Sir Nicholas Tempest of Stella in 1600. Tempest sold it in 1606 to Sir William Blakestone of Gibside and it became part of the Gibside estate.

Friarside Chapel has always stood in a romantic and secluded spot and has its fair share of legends. Treasure is rumoured to be hidden in its vicinity and a ghost is said to haunt the ruins. This ghost, however, was probably an ingenious invention of the illicit whisky distillers, who used to operate along the banks of the Derwent, in order to keep inquisitive eyes away from their activities. Despite this, not everyone avoided the area. A story appeared in the *Ladies' Newspaper* in London, dated 4 October 1851, which told how one morning a farmer found a 'grave' in the western part of the ruin, 8ft long, 4ft deep and about 2ft wide, that had clearly been dug by more than one person. Crowds came from far and wide to view this 'grave'. It transpired that a man called John Hepple from Winlaton had had a vivid recurring dream that the monks of old had buried some treasure inside the walls of the chapel. So convinced was he of its truth that he told a friend and together they dug the grave-shaped hole but found nothing of value. To the south west of the chapel lies Friarside Wood where locals used to bathe in a pool known as Holywell or Halliwell that was fed by a spring having water with a strong mineral content that turned plants to stone. The water was considered to have health-giving properties and the pool became a regular meeting place for young people on Sundays. It was also known as Pin Well since it became customary to drop a crooked pin into it before leaving. For many years, large quantities of pins could be seen at the bottom of a small pool into which the spring fell. After the South Garesfield Colliery had worked the coal seams in the area, the spring dried up and few, if any, traces of it remain.

Eight

Crookgate, The Fell and Barcus Close

Half a mile or so to the east of Burnopfield lies the small hamlet of Crookgate. Its name comes from the fact that a curved or crooked waggonway used to pass through it. Nowadays, Crookgate consists mainly of the Pack Horse public house and residential houses, many of which have been built in recent years. At one time there were two rows of miners' cottages opposite the front entrance to the Pack Horse, at the beginning of what is now called Fellside Road but which used to be known as Byermoor Lane. The old Pontop and Jarrow colliery railway line ran through Crookgate where there was a coal depot and several shops: Mr Woodcock had a corner shop and the Kyle family ran a general store. There also used to be a number of stone quarries in the Crookgate area. One of them, Wheatley's, provided the stones from which the 140ft-high Column to Liberty on the Gibside estate was cut between 1750 and 1757. The oldest houses still standing at Crookgate are in the area that includes Oak Terrace. This lies at the bottom of a steep bank, known as Crookgate Bank or Mile Bank, which leads on to Hobson and Pickering Nook. When the Pontop and Jarrow railway line was in operation there used to be a level crossing with a full set of gates halfway up the bank, close to a small terrace of houses known as Liddles Terrace, which was demolished some years ago.

There are two farms at Crookgate: Crookbank Farm and Crookfield Farm. In the 1930s, the Barcus Close Coal Company, which also had pits in the Bryan's Leap area and near the River Derwent, worked coal near Crookfield. About the same time, terraces of residential houses (all named after trees) were built at the top of Crookgate Bank in the area locally known as The Fell, after Fell Terrace behind which Burnopfield Co-operative Society used to have an abattoir. It also had a branch shop on the opposite side of the road. There are some former colliery managers' houses slightly further along the road towards Hobson at Bowesville, and there is a football field at the top of the lane that leads from the Fell over the old railway line down to the shops at Burnopfield. Towards the end of the nineteenth century, the Hancock family owned a sawmill on the Fell. When it closed the building became a YMCA and dances were held there before Burnopfield Co-operative Hall was built in 1893. It burned down in 1939.

The Pack Horse public house, 2000. This is one of the oldest public houses in the area and appears on the first series of Ordnance Survey maps published in 1856. The Pack Horse football team plays at the football field on the Fell.

Oak Terrace, Crookgate, c. 1910. The old terraces of miners cottages are just visible on the extreme right. There were sixteen cottages in all, built 'back-to-back' in two rows of eight with no space in between them.

A steam train passing Oak Terrace, *c.* 1910.

Burnopfield from Crookgate Bank, showing the old level crossing on Crookgate Bank, *c.* 1920. Prior to 1900, because of the severity of the incline on the section of the railway from Crookgate to Hobson Colliery, wagons were drawn along it using rope pulled by a stationary engine rather than being hitched behind a conventional steam locomotive. This arrangement proved to be very unsatisfactory, however, and also very dangerous. On 6 October 1879, the rope stuck and then flew up quickly, killing David Tweddle and laming Sarah Hunter. The stationary engine was abandoned in 1900 and locomotives were allowed to work the bank subject to certain conditions.

The level crossing on Crookgate Bank closed to allow a steam engine to pass, photographed in April 1968 by Trevor Ermel. The line closed later that year.

The Crookbank area, c. 1920. All these buildings have since been demolished.

Crookbank Farm, 2000. This is a working dairy farm owned by Robert Brown and his mother Belle Brown, who has lived there for sixty-five years.

Crookfield Farm, 2000, owned by Albert and Margaret Moss, includes part of the old Barcus Close Pit.

The old lane from the Fell down to Burnopfield, 2000.

The view from Barcus Close Lane, 2000. In recent years, new housing estates have been built at the Fell, extending some distance along Barcus Close Lane. This used to be a completely unspoilt country lane with Barcus Close Farm the only building in the area. Fortunately, however, much of its original charm still remains and impressive views towards Newcastle and the coast beyond can still be had from this vicinity.

Nine

Hobson and Pickering Nook

Hobson, which used to be known as Hobson Colliery or Burnopfield Colliery, is an old mining village; a pit shaft was first sunk there in 1725. Hobson is situated next to Pickering Nook on the road leading to the Fell and Crookgate. It is on high ground and commands fine views over the surrounding countryside. Streets of old stone-built houses still line the sides of the main road through the village, although some have been demolished over the years. Two of the oldest surviving buildings in the village are the former Primitive Methodist chapel and the Hobson Hotel. In pit villages like Hobson, before the days of public transport, family ties and relationships were many and strong. If two men started to fight it was not long before all their relations joined in and a riot would develop, with individual fights going on all over the place. Such an occurrence was described as 'Hell on'. As Hobson was the place where the wildest riots occurred, the saying 'Hell on at the Hobson' became associated with any such disturbance and was adopted into common parlance. No matter where such a riot took place it was described using the words: 'There's Hell on at the Hobson'.

Hobson used to be famous for its football team. A young man named Bruce, who was a mining engineer at the Hobson Colliery, formed the Hobson Wanderers Football Club in 1878. He had played football for Queen's Park in Scotland and trained the village lads well. In 1881 they reached the final of the County Cup where they played Sunderland, who were then an amateur team. The first match was a draw but Sunderland won the replay at Whitburn. Several players went from Hobson Wanderers to the top football clubs. Probably the most famous was 'Tantobie' Smith who played for Huddersfield when they beat Preston North End 1-0 at Stamford Bridge in the final of the FA Cup in the 1921/22 season, scoring the winning goal.

At nearby Pickering Nook there was a junior school, but this closed in 1982 and the building is now used as a private nursing and residential home. Pickering Nook probably got its name from a family called Pickering who used to own a blacksmith's shop beside Waggon Hill Farm. Nowadays, Pickering Nook consists mainly of residential houses apart from the former Pickering Nook garage, currently a motor home salesroom, which has stood at the junction of the Stanley road for many years.

A Hobson Colliery official, *c.* 1900. A bitter dispute over pay broke out at Hobson Colliery in December 1849, which resulted in many pitmen and their families being evicted from their homes. The remaining miners went on strike in sympathy. The dispute turned nasty and some of the striking miners, armed with guns, blew up the Hobson Colliery boilers with gunpowder. This made any further underground working impossible and had the desired effect of causing a serious loss of income to the mine owners.

Hobson Colliery Band, early 1900s.

Hobson Colliery workers parading along Front Street past the Hobson Hotel on Durham Big Meeting Day, c. 1960. The Hobson Hotel has been in existence for many years. A map of 1854 names its landlord as a George Nattrass. In the 1930s, Thomas Hall, the father of Norman Hall the haulage contractor, ran a butcher's shop at the Hobson, which now forms part of the restaurant at the Hobson Hotel.

Hobson Colliery in full production in April 1968, photographed by Trevor Ermel. It closed in July of that year. Before the mines were nationalized Hobson Colliery was owned and worked by John Bowes and partners. The colliery and its associated coke ovens and firebrick works used to provide employment for about 300 men and boys. In 1894, it was producing 140,000 tons of coal per annum. The owners of Hobson Colliery provided a Welfare Hall and sports grounds for their employees, including bowls, tennis, cricket and football, and all were played competitively at one time or another. When the pit closed in 1968, the colliery premises were converted into the modern industrial estate.

The former Hobson Primitive Methodist chapel at the end of Front Street, 2000. In around 1807, a Primitive Methodist group was formed at the Hobson. This grew and by 1859 they had built a chapel with seating for 140 at a cost of £142. Such was the increase in membership that a new gothic-style chapel with seating for 250 was built in 1890 at a cost of £750. The first service was held in the new chapel on Whit Sunday, 16 May 1891. In 1934, a Sunday school was added at the rear of the main building and this operated for many years. Because of dwindling attendances, the final service was held on Sunday 22 September 1974. The building is now used as a kitchen and bathroom showroom.

Hobson Golf Club, 2000. The eighteen-hole golf course at Hobson has a fine clubhouse, which was completed in 1980. It has a very distinctive roof, which can be seen from miles around. Jack Ord, seen above on the putting green, has been the professional at the club since 1981.

Hobson Wanderers, *c.* 1900.

Hobson Colliery cricket team, 1935.

Hobson Bowling Club, *c.* 1940.

Mattie Baker (who later managed the Grand cinema in Burnopfield) was born at Hobson and is shown here surrounded by his four aunts: Bette, Hannah, Hilda and May Wales.

Ten

Byermoor

Byermoor, one mile or so east of Burnopfield, is a village where coal mining has been carried on for hundreds of years. It is much older than Burnopfield, and is mentioned in the Bolden Book (1183) as 'Biermore' or 'Beechemoor', which means 'Bare Moors'. Over the years, various families owned it and by the seventeenth century it was the property of the Harrisons, who also owned a house at Bryan's Leap. At the start of the eighteenth century, the rights to mine coal at Byermoor were owned by Sir Thomas Clavering, who opened a colliery there. Subsequently, the colliery and the mineral rights were acquired by the Bowes family of Gibside, who became very wealthy through its involvement with the coal trade.

In October 1956, Mr E. Barkley and Mr Bart Waites, two miners in a Byermoor drift broke through into an old working and found a stoneware jug showing the bearded smiling face of an old man. From the colliery records, the old workings where the jug was found were pre-1759. The mystery jug was sent to the Laing Art Gallery in Newcastle where it aroused great interest. It was identified as one of the Bellarmine jugs that had been made in quantities from 1550 to 1700, first in Flanders and then in England. This one had probably been made in Fulham around 1670. These jugs portrayed the face of the famous Cardinal Bellarmine (1542-1621) who was the leader of the Roman Catholic side in the controversy with the Protestants. References to these jugs appear in old plays including Bartholomew Fair by Ben Johnson. Cardinal Bellarmine was on the church tribunal before which the astronomer Galileo was called to justify his theory that the Earth was a satellite of the sun and not at the centre of the universe. The story is well known: how Galileo submitted to the will of the Church but under his breath murmured 'Yet it does move'.

The old mining village was demolished not long after Byermoor Colliery closed on 31 January 1968. Modern Byermoor consists of the Roman Catholic church of the Sacred Heart and its presbytery, the Sacred Heart Primary School and the red-brick housing estate originally owned by the council but many of whose houses are now owner-occupied.

Grove Terrace United Methodist Free Church, c. 1900. The old miners' cottages at Byermoor and the Sacred Heart Roman Catholic church are in the background. Byermoor Colliery consisted of the colliery itself, the manager's house and a few rows of pit cottages. These were Double Row, New Row, Furnace Row and Pit Row. All were built between 1865 and 1890. Above the former site of Double Row is a football field, which belongs to the Catholic school.

New Row, Byermoor, 16 August 1968. On the main road, not far from New Row, was the Mission Room or 'tin church', as it was known, a corrugated iron building, which was an outpost of St Cuthbert's Anglican church at Marley Hill. It can be seen in the previous photograph and was demolished in the late 1950s. Between the Mission Room and New Row was 'The Green', which was used during the 1926 General Strike for playing quoits. Below New Row there were some quarries where illegal 'pitch and toss' schools used to take place on Sunday mornings. Hundreds of pounds changed hands and there was always a look-out stationed on top of the quarry to give ample warning for the schools to scatter if the village bobby was sighted.

An outside toilet or 'netty'. In the early days, every miner's cottage in Byermoor and the surrounding villages had a netty. This took the form of a 'muck midden' having an oblong wooden lid, in the centre of which was a round hole with a separate wooden lid. The fire ashes were emptied into the midden. It was not unknown for someone to fall into the midden when the oblong lid was left up by mistake.

A 'muck midden'. The 'toilet paper' was newspaper cut into squares, skewered at the corner and hung on a string on the door. At Byermoor, once a week the midden-man, with a bright coloured handkerchief wrapped round his nose and mouth, called at all the houses in the street. Accompanied by his horse and cart and shovel, he would clean the middens by way of a small doorway set in the outside wall under the toilets.

The church of the Sacred Heart, Byermoor, 2000. The foundation stone was laid on 12 September 1875 and Bishop Chadwick officially opened the church on 8 October 1876. It came to fruition largely through the efforts of Father Patrick Thomas Mathews, who was the parish priest at Byermoor from 1869 to 1879. The church stands near the top of one of the highest hills in the area and commands fine views of the Derwent Valley and the distant Cheviot Hills on a clear day. Adjoining the church is the presbytery, which was built in 1882 when Father John Wilson was the parish priest. He was also responsible for the building of the school behind the church in 1883.

The Sacred Heart Roman Catholic Voluntary Aided Primary School, Byermoor, 2000. Currently, the school has five teachers, including the head teacher Mrs Sands, and about ninety pupils.

The statue of the Crucifixion in Byermoor churchyard was erected in 1934 and carries the following inscription: 'This cross was made and erected (figure from Italian Tyrol) by the people of Byermoor Parish. Blessed March 25th 1934 by Fr. Austin Pickering PP. Stone base and surrounding added in 1952 – R.I.P.'

The former colliery manager's house, 2000. All that remains of Byermoor Colliery are some of the old surface buildings and the former colliery manager's house that used to be attached to the end of New Row. In the old colliery office is the original louvre window through which the miners received their pay packets.

The red-brick housing estate, Byermoor, which was built in the 1930s. The names of the Crescents in the estate all have local associations: Bowes, Gibside, Ravensworth and Strathmore.

From the red-brick housing estate a lane runs to the old High Marley Hill School, shown above, which was built in 1875. The school buildings were taken over in 1961 by the firm of C. Hetherington, garden wholesale suppliers.

Eleven

Schooldays

The first school in Burnopfield was probably run by a Methodist preacher, William Hopper, at the house where he lived in Sheephill from 1746 to 1748. However, this was rare since, even by the start of the nineteenth century, education for the masses was almost non-existent. This changed when churches and local mine owners began to take an interest in education. The upstairs room above the stable of the 1775 Methodist chapel was used as a day school for many years. A colliery church school opened at Lintz Colliery in 1863 and a day school began under the Grove Terrace Methodist Free church around 1870. Towards the end of the nineteenth century, three new schools were built, which will be remembered fondly by many of the older residents in the area. The first was Burnopfield National School in 1872, followed by Pickering Nook Board School in 1892 and Leazes Board School in 1894. All three took children between the ages of five and fourteen and, by 1913, despite a total capacity of almost 900, they were overflowing. This seems remarkable given that, in the year 2000 with many more houses in the area, only Burnopfield Primary School and Nursery with 350 primary pupils and 52 nursery pupils is considered to be sufficient.

Pupils at the schools could transfer to a grammar school if they passed the Eleven-Plus examination. Burnopfield Secondary Modern School opened in 1933 to take the unsuccessful eleven-plus children in the area. The first headmaster was Mr Edward ('Ned') Bell, who in his younger days had played football for Sunderland. He had to resign after a few months because of ill health, and Mr Mackerell from Easington replaced him. Mr Jack Uren became headmaster in 1956 and, when major educational re-organization took place in the area in 1968 he took all the children to Shield Row Secondary Modern School. Burnopfield Secondary Modern School building became Burnopfield Junior and Infants' School, taking all the children from the National School and the Leazes Board School. Mr Morgan, the headmaster of the National School, retired and Mr Beckham, the headmaster of Leazes Board School, became headmaster of the new school. In 1976, a new building saw the school split into separate junior and infants' schools. It is now Burnopfield Primary School and Nursery, the current headmaster being Mr John Rymaszewski.

Lintz School, c. 1880. On 20 July 1863, a colliery church school was opened at Lintz Colliery, in the aptly named School Street. A local coal owner, Mr Gooch of Leazes Hall, had the school built at a cost of £200. The first headmaster was a Mr Tait. Every Monday morning, each pupil had to pay a fee of twopence for the week. When the school closed in 1893, it was converted into two houses and was later extended to form the long since demolished Miners' Institute.

Burnopfield Masonic Lodge, formerly Burnopfield National School, in 2000. The school was built opposite Burnopfield Methodist chapel on a site given by the Marquis of Bute and with donations from the church at Leazes and the Local Authority. It was opened in 1872 and could cater for 200 mixed children and 140 infants. It closed in 1968 and is now used as a Masonic Lodge. The first headmaster was Mr Hogarth who was an enthusiastic cricketer for Burnopfield, and the last was Mr 'Johnny' Morgan.

A Burnopfield National School class, *c.* 1890. The headmaster was Mr Hogarth. All writing in the schools was done on slates using squeaky slate pencils; it was many years before pens dipped in inkwells for writing in proper exercise books became available. The school day usually began with mental arithmetic, and from every classroom came the sound of 'Twice one are two, twice two are four...' and so on. Knowledge of the tables was a must; there were no calculators then.

A Burnopfield National School class, *c.* 1916. Other subjects taught were history and geography (both chiefly about the British Empire), music (mainly singing the 'scales'), and physical training, or 'drill' as it was called, which consisted chiefly of standing in the aisles between the desks doing 'arms bend, knees stretch' exercises. Practical subjects, like domestic science, woodwork and science, were unheard of.

A class at Burnopfield National School, *c.* 1918. From left to right, back row: Mr Middleton (headmaster), Amy Lowe, Cecil Metcalf, Teddy Barcus, -?-, Elsie Young, Jennie Stevenson, Cyril Atkinson, Lance Tinkler, Evelyn Tinkler, Vera Spoor, Katy Largue, Lily Carter, Martha Handcock, Cissie Stephenson, Miss Elizabeth (Betty) Spurr (class teacher). Middle row: -?-, John Humble, Edna Churcher, Tommie Underwood, Freddie Stevenson, Helen Forster, Joe Clark, Doris Ord, Agnes Brewis, Lilian Iley, Nat Spurr, Eva Morley, Annie Johnson, Evelyn Armstrong. Front row: Gladys Lowe, -?-, Jimmy French, Tommy Hughes, Winston Davis, Tommy Bailey, Eddie Lever, Lizzie Hughes, -?-, Eileen Robson, Tommy Bland, Robbie Hudspith, -?-, -?-. In front, with the board: Billy Bibby, Lance Robson.

A Burnopfield National School class, *c.* 1950, with the headmaster Mr Lamb (at the extreme left).

120

Burnopfield National School class of 1960 showing those who had passed their Eleven-Plus. From left to right, back row: Barry Richardson, Billy Brabban, Joe Lumsden, Billy Trewick. Front row: Susan Matthews, Patricia Minto, Pamela Baker, Eileen Johnson.

The staff of Burnopfield Infants' School when it split from the Junior School in 1976. From left to right, back row: Jennifer Parker, Thelma Jude (nursery nurse), Lydia Patterson, Muriel Williams (secretary). Front row: Jennifer Armstrong (*née* Lumsden), Audrey Grant (*née* Ovington), Nancy Nevin (head teacher), Christine Maddison, Marion Cookson.

The next generation: pupils of the first nursery class at Burnopfield Primary School, 1992. The members of staff are, from left to right: Miss Craig (NNEB), Mrs Hole (teacher) and Mrs Smith (NNEB).

Pickering Nook Board School, c. 1980. This opened in 1892 and could cater for 144 mixed and 65 infants. Mr G.R. Smith was its first headmaster; he had previously been in charge of the school under the Grove Terrace United Methodist church. When Pickering Nook School closed in 1982 its headmistress was Mrs Doreen Elliott and the thirty-three children still on the school roll were transferred to other schools in the area. As a memento, Mrs Elliott presented each of them with a miniature miner's lamp inscribed 'Pickering Nook School 1892-1982'. For a short time afterwards, the school building became a craft centre but in 1989 it was altered to its current use as a private residential and nursing home.

A Pickering Nook School class, between 1900 and 1910.

The Leazes Board School, *c.* 1894. It opened on 8 January 1894 and could cater for 250 mixed and 100 infants. The Leazes School was built to replace the old Lintz Colliery School, which closed on 21 December 1893. Mr Richard ('Dick') Abbott, who had been headmaster of Lintz Colliery School since 1887, became the first headmaster of the Leazes School and all the six staff and 178 children from Lintz Colliery School moved there with him.

A Leazes Board School class, *c.* 1910, with the headmaster, Mr Abbott. There was a scheme whereby children could leave school at the age of twelve rather than fifteen, if they passed a 'Labour Examination' by showing that they had reached a sufficiently high standard in the three Rs (Reading, Writing and Arithmetic). Family incomes were so limited in those days that many parents took advantage of this scheme. The boys usually went to the mines and the girls 'to place': that is, to domestic service, placed is some well-to-do person's house.

Leazes Board School class, *c.* 1920, with the headmaster Mr Abbott. Mr Abbott had quite a reputation as a stern disciplinarian. After Mr Abbott, the headmasters were Mr Close, Mr Gladstone and finally Mr George Beckham. One of the longest-serving and best-loved teachers at the school was Miss J. Leadbitter who taught the infants for forty-four years. The Leazes School closed on 19 July 1968 and is now used as Burnopfield Youth and Community Centre.

The Modern School, Burnopfield, c. 1950. The building just to the left of the lamp-post is the Constitutional Club, which was demolished in 1957 when the building of the present Burnopfield Gospel Fellowship church began.

The first day at Burnopfield Modern School, 1933. The teachers who can just be seen in the doorway from left to right are Mr Bell (headmaster), Miss Lamb and Miss Freek.

Burnopfield Modern School staff, *c.* 1940. From left to right, back row: Mr Hall, Mr Ramsey, Mr Nesbitt, Mr Grey, Mr Foggin, Mr Watchman, Mr Templeton. Front row: Miss Johnston, Miss Huck, Mr Mackerell (headmaster), Miss Buglass, Miss Lamb, Miss Freek.

Mr
Grev

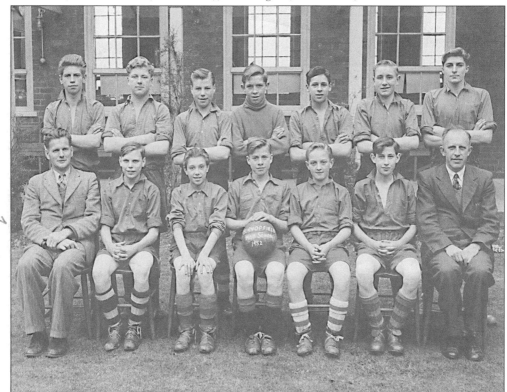

Burnopfield Modern School football team, 1952.

The Burnopfield Modern School production of *The Mikado*, 1951.

Some of the girls of Burnopfield Modern School taking part in a school show, *c.* 1965.

Burnopfield Modern School sports teams of 1959. In the middle of the back row is Frank Spraggon, who played football for Middlesbrough. On the extreme right of the middle row is David Elliott who played football for Sunderland.

Burnopfield Modern School staff, circa 1960. From left to right, back row: Mr Angus Robinson, Mr Benny Hindmarsh, Mr Norman Williams, Mr Jim Moss, -?-. Front row: Mr Seaman, Mrs Rowell, Mr Jack Uren (headmaster), Miss Hilda Buglass, Mr Bob Grey, -?-, Mr Frank Brabban.